Documents in Canadian Architecture

SAUCIER + PERROTTE ARCHITECTES

Tuns Press
Faculty of Architecture and Planning
Dalhousie University
P.O. Box 1000
Halifax, Nova Scotia
Canada B3J 2X4
tunspress.dal.ca

Saucier + Perrotte Architectes 1995 - 2002
Editor: Brian Carter
Design: Stéphane Huot
Cover design: Saucier + Perrotte
Production: Donald Westin
Printing: Friesens

Canadian Cataloguing in Publication Data
Saucier + Perrotte Architectes / Saucier + Perrotte; Brian Carter, ed.
(Documents in Canadian Architecture)
Includes some text in French.
ISBN 0-929112-46-6
1. Architecture – Canada – 20th century. 2. Saucier + Perrotte (Firm)
I. Carter, Brian, 1942- II. Saucier + Perrotte (Firm)
III. Title: Saucier + Perrotte Architectes. IV. Series.

NA749.S29S29 2004   720'.971'09049   C2002-905158-4

Contents

Foreword

The work of Saucier + Perrotte is some of the most searching, radical work in Canada and holds much raw energy of ideas. It is surprising partly because of the contrast with its context. Québec is a place of the greatest historical presence in Canada. The work's freshness and contrast is the more stark for that. This is a place of rich heritage and a well-established approach. If there is a connection between this work and its historical setting, that connection is at the deepest cultural level where attitudes to culture and life are embodied in a formal tradition with its own native canons and conventions.

It is tempting, in such a distinct setting, to try to see this work in terms of what is expected from most architecture: contextualism and harmony. That would also be true to generally accepted dogmas in architecture. But to do so, one would have to stretch the argument and disregard the more evident quality of this work. Collége Gérald-Godin is not "contextual." Théâtre d'Aujourd'hui is made of material fragments that remain fragments in tense contrast to the compositional harmony of the whole. Saucier + Perrotte's design for the Canadian Embassy in Berlin was the most daring of their projects. In the face of the very complexity and contrasting demands of that project it seemed that their design had found its natural architectural programme. It made one reflect that perhaps they sense a similar essential disharmony in any programme of our time and search to guard it from pre-emptive ideas of composition and order.

In our critical attempt to understand any body of work, references to previous ideas and analogies with other fields come to mind. But no such reference reaches the core of the character and quality of this work. Rather, it seems not to be ordered by any pre-formulated position. It exists as an original body of work in its own right. This work is not a reconstruction of a given vocabulary – it is in search of a different vocabulary altogether. It comprises a series of compositions of materials, colour, texture and light, each perceptible in its own right as well as part of a more complex composition. These aspects are inherently bound together in single building materials and volumes. The work seems to follow a pure architectural / aesthetic thesis about the possibility of isolating these aspects from one another: they are decomposed to emphasize their possible independence from their natural state. The fact of their inherent unity can be defined and the richness of that unity can thus be revealed. The result would be like breaking open an atom and releasing the energy that binds its parts together. This seems to be the search behind the quality of the work in this book – it is radical.

Essy Baniassad

Absence /separation /difference

Some years ago it was suggested that one characteristic of modern architecture in French Canada was its "apparent absence." In the context of that apparent absence, it was noted that "even the place as such has to be located: French Canada is Québec."[1] This claim highlighted a perception that has tended to persist.

The apparent absence of French Canada and its modern architecture could be seen as a consequence of isolation – an isolation that can be traced back to the founding of the territory. After establishing the first cluster of fortified buildings at Cap Diamant in 1608 Champlain had to embark on an arduous campaign to transform his tentative outpost of New France into a colony. And, almost fifty years later, when a group of French religious mystics was inspired to build a missionary city in the wilderness they chose a site that was eventually to become the city of Montréal. In 1759, these settlers of French Canada were cut off from their origins by the British and the consequent isolation was further compounded by subsequent demands for the autonomy of the territory by an all-powerful Catholic Church. More recently provincial government policies have constructed other confines, such as the required use of the French language in commerce, administration and education, that have contributed further to the separateness of Québec.

But while these events of history, combined with the impact of climate and geography, have been significant they have also helped to build a rich and distinct French-Canadian culture. It is a culture with distinguished literary traditions and where lively arts communities are actively working in theatre, film and performance. Architecture and design are also a part of this cultural richness – a richness that has been enhanced by the presence of the Canadian Centre for Architecture in Montréal and a professional community of architects in the province that is the largest in Canada.[2]

The work of Saucier + Perrotte is deeply rooted in French Canada. Both architects were born in the countryside north of Québec, educated locally and studied architecture at Université Laval. After graduating in 1982 they moved to Montréal, formed their own office in 1988 and, for the first ten years, all of their work was in French Canada. However, as well as receiving commissions to design interiors for apartments, restaurants and shops – work that frequently forms the bedrock of emerging architectural practices – they were also invited to design new facilities for Montréal's lively arts communities. These projects, to build and enrich French-Canadian culture, were for provincially funded theatre, film and performance. With modest budgets they designed several theatres that, albeit small, were technically complex and designed to fit within existing buildings in the city.

The Théâtre d'Aujourd'hui, a 300-seat flexible space planned for an experimental theatre company committed to the production of Québécoise drama, was an almost invisible project. Designed in 1990 it utilised a space within an existing residential building on Rue St-Denis to create new performance areas and public facilities. While this theatre was hardly discernable from the street, another commission to redesign facilities for Québec's oldest theatre company, the Théâtre du Rideau Vert, was more obvious. It required the creation of a new auditorium to seat 426 people, together with expanded front-of-house facilities and an entrance on Rue St-Denis.

These designs entailed the creation of spaces that satisfied the stringent requirements of theatrical production, acoustics and public access. They were also inspired by the spectacle implicit in the design and operation of spaces for performance. As a result newly formed auditoria were conspicuously shaped while the staircases, ramps and lifts that inevitably had to be added were designed as obvious sculptural pieces. The architects also used these projects as a basis to experiment with materials – experiments that developed a palette of stained and molded timber, polished concrete, plywood, different types of glass, gun-metal and weathering steel. Prompted by economy, these materials were often used in their natural and untreated states.

These modest theatres were also used primarily at night. As a consequence the architects explored the use of both colour and artificial light in their designs to devise ways of defining and distorting space, create different atmospheres and emphasise the spectacle of movement with the limited means that were available. It was in designing these projects, with their explorations of the experiential and illusory qualities of space, colour, light and material, that Saucier + Perrotte's work developed distinct sensual qualities.

Their scheme for the Montréal-based troupe Carbone 14 in 1993 was not only to provide a more ambitious range of facilities but also required the complete transformation of a large redundant factory. The troupe wanted to use this industrial building in the east end of Montréal because it not only offered a range of different sized spaces but was near the communities that the troupe served. In planning this centre for performance and the arts, the architects developed a design that emphasised a distinct ambiguity between the existing and the new. Externally, new openings were formed within the clearly expressed grid of the industrial frame. Glazed, clad in stone or infilled with panels of weathering steel, these openings and insertions clearly denoted the building's changed use. Colour was assertively introduced and parts of the building became backdrops for the large-scale projection of images created by artists. Floor slabs within the four-storey-high reinforced concrete framed building were cut away, creating large volumes to accommodate public spaces and the insertion of new stairs and ramps. The sculptural form of the structure and the presence of the frame were conspicuously revealed and contrasted with the lightness of new glass screens and metal ramps. Walls that were added were emphatically thin, dramatically folded or pierced to align with existing openings and to frame new ones.

The Cinémathèque Québécoise, completed four years later, advanced these ideas. It consisted of an art and film centre with two cinemas, exhibition galleries, an archive, film school and a café. Planned within a former school on Boulevard de Maisonneuve Est – a major street in the centre of Montréal – the project also brought back into use an adjacent two-storey brick building that was vacant. By skillfully re-planning these two buildings and connecting them with a third building that was new, the design focused the development around a new entrance and public courtyard that reconfigured this part of the city and extended the public realm.

This third building was literally layered over the existing. It was both a physical layering that built on the idea of the cinema screen and an illusory one that referenced film. The new building, housing the main entrance into the Cinémathèque, was planned to provide a series of places to view the moving image while ingeniously exploring one of the inherent qualities of film and cinema. Film fuses light and the image with movement and time – a unique aspect of the medium that the critic Susan Sontag effectively described when she wrote that "movies and television programs light up walls, flicker and go out."[3] This project investigated those changing aspects of light. It also highlights the ambiguous relationships between image, viewer and viewed. Consequently, the main entrance façade on the street also becomes a screen where images are projected at the scale of the city and viewed by passers-by, whilst the entrance hall itself has been designed as a cinema. On entering this space the visitor becomes both viewer and viewed as images of people entering are projected on the screen to reference that momentary lighting up of walls and flicker of the film itself.

Whilst the commission to design an extension to the Faculty of Design at the Université de Montréal also involved Saucier + Perrotte in planning new alongside old, this particular building was to house a radically different program. In addition, the project was part of a more expansive landscape. Conceived as an addition to the symmetrical figure of an existing four-storey building, it marked both the edge of the campus and a face to the city. The new five-storey building consisted of a T-shaped addition housing design studios, offices, a library and seminar rooms. It was located alongside an existing building so as to form two outdoor courtyards.

Cinémathèque Québécoise

The scheme improved existing facilities and in particular created a new main entrance with a sculptural auditorium alongside. These changes were signaled on the street by a "plaque" – a weathering steel screen applied to the external facade of the existing stone building. The project also sought to re-connect the Faculty back into the infrastructure of the campus. To do this it was placed astride a major pedestrian route that extended through the campus to Mont Royal – a peak and park that have a powerful presence in both campus and city. The new studios were planned on four floors and fully glazed, creating a lightness and transparency that literally revealed the activities of the Faculty to the campus. Lifting the new building up off the ground allowed the existing path to not only engage the building but to connect to the new courtyards and adjacent streets. As a result the School became a landmark on the campus – a gigantic window, that is an overlook by day, and a lantern along the route at night. While earlier projects of Saucier + Perrotte tended to be preoccupied with the design of discrete spaces contained and hidden within other worlds, this scheme was conspicuously shaped by both the translation of the building program and its setting in the wider landscape.

These projects extended the scope of the work of Saucier + Perrotte; however, it was still confined within French Canada. With their selection as competitors in an invited national competition to design a new Canadian Embassy in Germany in 1999, this was to change. The site for the building was on a corner on Leipziger Platz in the centre of Berlin. It had a narrow frontage and, in addition, the city planning regulations defined the height of the building, its fenestration and the materials from which it could be constructed. By proposing a scheme that formed an inner courtyard, open to the sky and clearly visible from the street, Saucier + Perrotte developed a design that responded to the particular requirements of the city while proposing a space at the heart of the building that made specific reference to Canada. The plan that they devised ingeniously combined requirements for a building that was to be civic and private, open and closed, contextual yet emblematic. The space of this new courtyard was devised to provide insights into the country and its characteristics. By incorporating water, rock and trees in the design they referenced the importance of the natural landscape that is a fundamental part of the Canadian psyche. Information and colour were also added. With these evocations Saucier + Perrotte's scheme promised a talisman at the centre of the new embassy. Although the commission was eventually awarded to another competitor, Saucier + Perrotte's proposal created a heightened awareness of their work, and as a result they were considered for other significant projects elsewhere across the country.

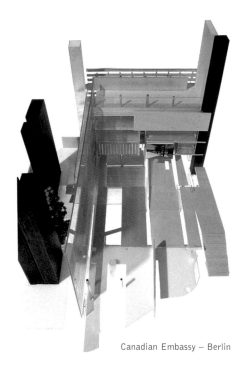

Canadian Embassy – Berlin

Saucier + Perrotte were successful in winning commissions to design the Perimeter Institute – a research facility in Waterloo, a residential building for New College in the heart of Toronto and an Information Technology Centre at the University of Toronto's Erindale Campus. While some of these larger projects are yet to be fully completed, other smaller projects have continued to provide valuable testing grounds. In designing the interiors of Orbite – a tiny salon – they explored the use of light and colour in ways that recall R.M. Schindler's hidden light sources, while the new interiors designed for their own studio clearly reference the space-making sculpture of Richard Serra. Gilles Saucier talks enthusiastically about the work of both Serra and Schindler. The simultaneous consideration of building, materiality and landscape is one aspect of that work that holds his interest while Serra's enthusiasm for the intrinsic qualities of materials and Schindler's experimental treatments of concrete, metals and wood continues to inspire.

The scheme for the Collège Gérald-Godin most effectively demonstrates the inspiration and synthesis of these ideas. The college, located in Sainte-Geneviève – a French-speaking hamlet outside Montréal, now engulfed by suburbs – has been built on a site that overlooks the Rivière-des-Prairies. A former monastery, the hamlet's most prominent landmark, had been abandoned and was identified by the provincial government as the place to establish a new college. This college was not only to re-affirm the French-Canadian character of the place but also to encourage residents to complete their education in their native language. The existing five-storey, stone-faced building was undistinguished. Constructed in 1933, it was closed and formidable in character. With the completion of this scheme it has been radically transformed. Teachers' offices, administrative facilities and a library, ingeniously fitted high up into the space of the former chapel, have been planned within the existing building while other major spaces have been added in new buildings alongside. Generous spaces for sport, theatre and the arts significantly expand educational facilities in the region. However, in an effort to reduce the impact of these large volumes Saucier + Perrotte planned the facilities below ground, yet connected to the existing and new buildings. This has, in turn, enabled them to shape the land in ways that re-orient the development. Now the buildings of the college are more open and also generously connected to the river. The roofs of the underground spaces create a series of landscaped terraces that form a foundation for new classrooms above. Lanterns on those terraces are sculpted in weathering steel and scoop daylight into the spaces below. The new classroom block has been conspicuously shaped,

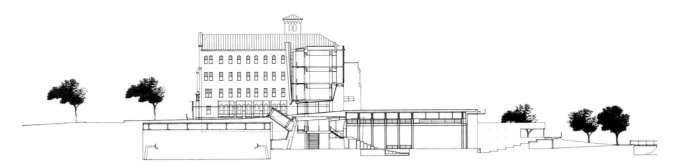

Collège Gérald-Godin

coloured and stridently patterned to form a sculpted object that is a striking contrast to the formal stone faces of the former monastery. It clearly signals a new identity for this historic place. While the scheme successfully transforms the existing through the ingenious introduction of new uses and the addition of conspicuously different buildings, it is also compelling in the way that it engages those buildings with the landscape.

Saucier + Perrotte have been developing an architectural approach that is spatially complex. It is rich with the subtleties of material, the details of their assembly and the manipulation of light. And, while clearly rooted in the context of a distinctive regional culture, their work increasingly shows the influence of other references and registers difference. It has been suggested that today the consideration of difference is focused on expressions of identity – race, gender, nationality and class. However, for Aristotle it meant something more. As Richard Sennett has noted, Aristotle included "also the experience of doing different things, of acting in divergent ways which do not fit neatly together" and went on to suggest that, while all modern designers of cities claim to subscribe to this Aristotelian principle, "if in the same space different persons or activities are merely concentrated, but each remains isolated and segregated, diversity loses its force. Differences have to interact."[4] Saucier + Perrotte are increasingly provoking such interaction in their work and successfully making an architecture of significance that now extends beyond the confines of French Canada.   Brian Carter

1. Melvin Charney, "Quebec's Modern Architecture," in Documents in Canadian Architecture, edited by Geoffrey Simmins (Peterborough, ON: Broadview Press, 1992), 268.

2. Information supplied by the provincial associations of architects in Canada in indicated that in 2002 there were 2,700 registered architects in Quebec, compared to 2,300 in Ontario and 1,400 in British Columbia, with approximately 7,500 in the whole of Canada.

3. Susan Sontag, On Photography (Harmondswoth: Penguin Books, 1979), 3.

4. Richard Sennett, The Spaces of Democracy, 1998 Raoul Wallenberg Lecture (Ann Arbor: University of Michigan, 1998), 19–20.

[2004 – 2003]

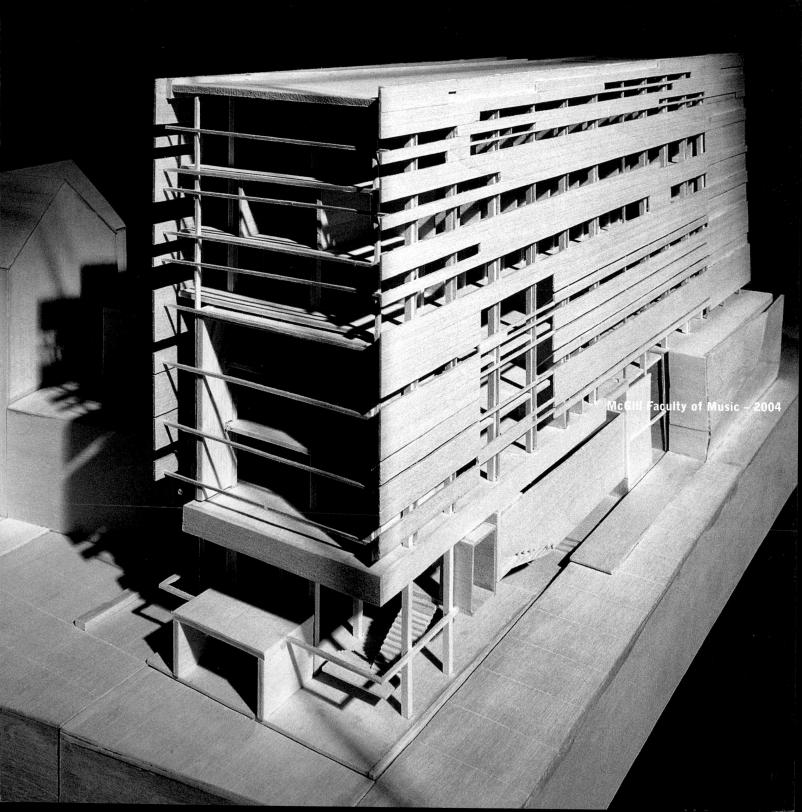

McGill Faculty of Music – 2004

CCIT – 2004

Perimeter Institute – 2004

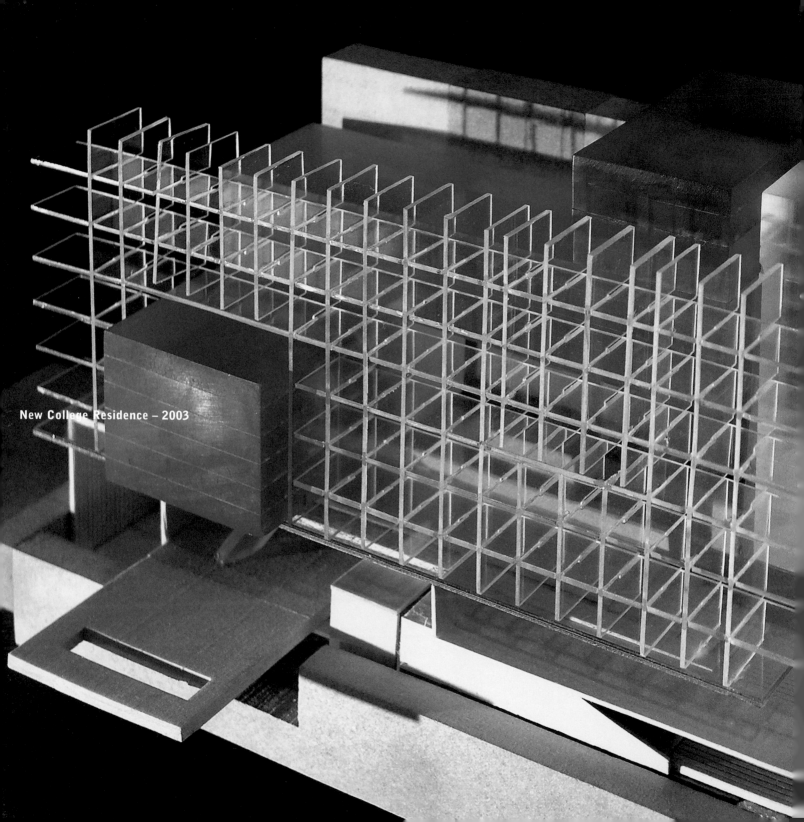

New College Residence – 2003

Dance and Theatre | In keeping with the spirit of reinvention and experimentation that characterizes the work of the Montréal-based performance troupe, the design of the new theatre, offices and practice studios for Carbone 14 was an exercise in transformation. Rather than selecting a site in the downtown hub, the troupe chose to adapt an existing factory in a working class area in east-end Montreal. | The tectonic strategy for transforming the factory was two-pronged. The massive concrete structure of the existing building was exposed, and it inspired an "invented archaeology" in which new concrete elements, such as the board-formed concrete wall of a ramp that connects the lobby and foyer, render ambiguous what is new and what is old. In contrast, other new construction was designed to be light and delicate to create a counterpoint to the weight and texture of the existing structure. This building contains all public gathering areas at ground level as well as support and administrative functions above. Two new added volumes contain the practice studio and a 450-seat theatre. A courtyard was created between the existing factory and these new additions. This intimate exterior space, which is accessible from the main hall, the practice studio and the foyer, can be used by both performers and audience. | An existing tall chimney adjacent to the four-storey brick factory becomes a landmark for the new theatre. With a raised box, clad in glass and weathering steel, it identifies the main entrance to the complex. At this entrance a ramp leading to the main doors changes into a bridge that overlooks the café in the old boiler room. An attenuated promenade leads the audience from Rue Visitation into the building. A ticket booth flanks a long open-plan entrance hall that is defined by exposed concrete columns. A double-height yellow plaster wall marks a light steel stair that leads to the second floor foyer, and an expansive glass wall provides views over the city. | The new performance hall is accessible from the street through a linear foyer that intersects the lobby and overlooks the courtyard. This hall is a flexible space that permits a variety of configurations through its planning and the use of modular seating. A series of steel bridges between the trusses allow easy access to lighting, and exposed structural steel trusses echo the former uses of the factory. **Montréal 1995**

1 former jam factory
2 new theatre
3 entrance
4 courtyard
5 bridge over side entrance

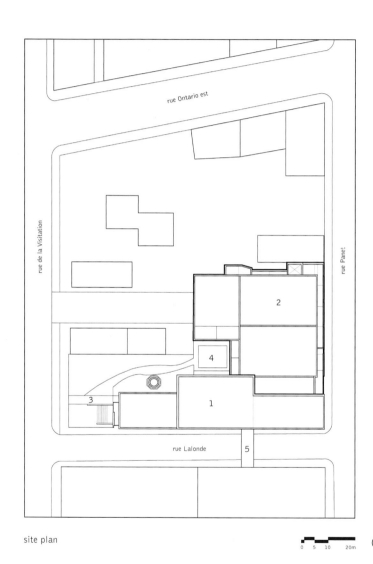

site plan

rue Ontario est

rue de la Visitation

rue Pane?

rue Lalonde

0 5 10   20m

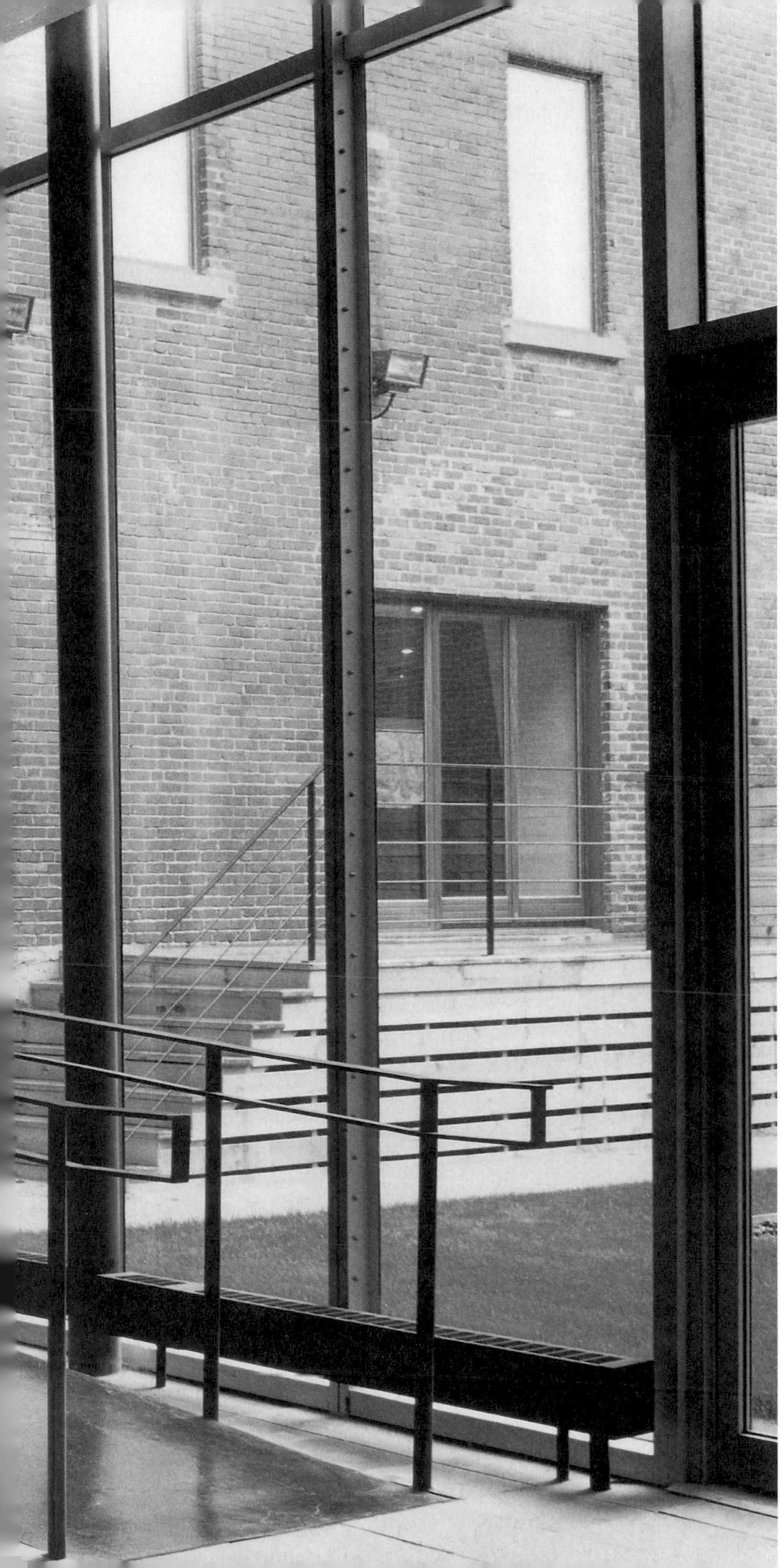

1 entrance
2 main hall / foyer
3 coat check
4 ticket booth
5 450-seat theatre
6 practice studio
7 café (below)
8 exterior courtyard
9 second floor foyer
10 offices

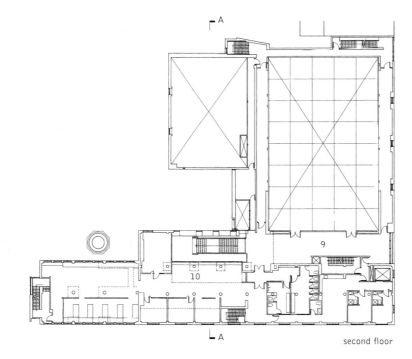

second floor

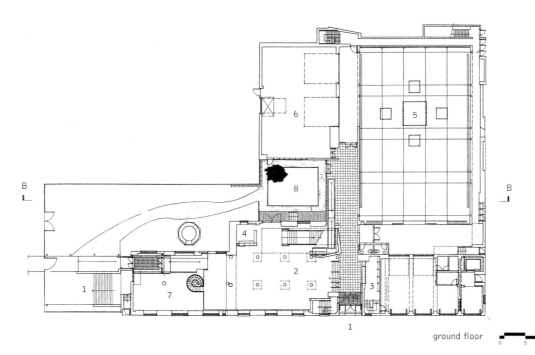

ground floor

0   5   10m

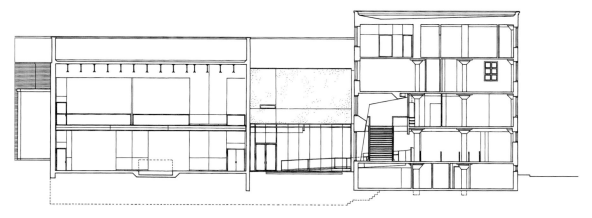

section A: through main hall and practice studios

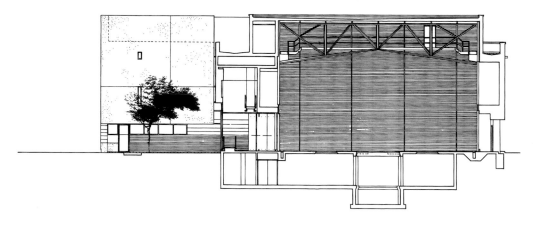

section B: through main theatre and courtyard

0 1   5   10m

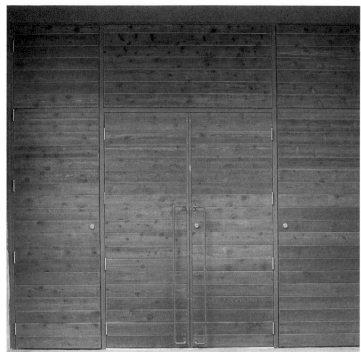

Faculty of Design | The conceptual approach to the design of this project uses light and landscape as foci for academic study. The design seeks to emphasize the creative energy generated by the Faculty of Design and project it into the campus and the city. A series of existing spaces were renovated and linked to new spaces constructed for the studios and critique rooms. Two new prismatic volumes have been added to the existing building, with the largest enclosing a sunken court. A glazed screen brings natural light into the studios and makes the activity of the studio a part of the urban landscape to the south. The studio building, planned on five floors, is encased in a metallic skin to control natural light along its south elevation. | A second volume forms a passage that connects the campus and Mont Royal. This passage provides access from Côte Ste-Catherine to the common areas and to the mountain beyond. Critique rooms and exhibition halls located along this route introduce life and energy to create a layout that favours the interchange of ideas between the different schools in the building. As the facilities had to remain in use while the construction was underway, the design was developed to insert the new program elements without disruption. The various departments still encircle the main courtyard, and the central circulation spine links the studios to the rest of the school's functions. | A series of discrete interventions transform the north façade, which fronts onto Côte Ste-Catherine. A plaque of weathering steel is placed over the main entrance and marks the terminus of the central circulation route. To the east of the entrance tall glass elements spanning the full four storeys punctuate the rhythm of the openings on the facade and reveal the new auditorium. Each emphasizes the existing geometry of the building while responding to the reconfigured functions within. | The newly constructed landscape of the courtyard creates a common ground for the complex. Stone – as bedrock, foundation, stone fill, stone wall, and carved stone – is combined with soil and wood to create a landscape for meditation and to connect the seasonal and scholastic rhythms. **Montréal 1996**

UNIVERSITÉ DE MONTRÉAL

1 main campus
2 existing building
3 new wing

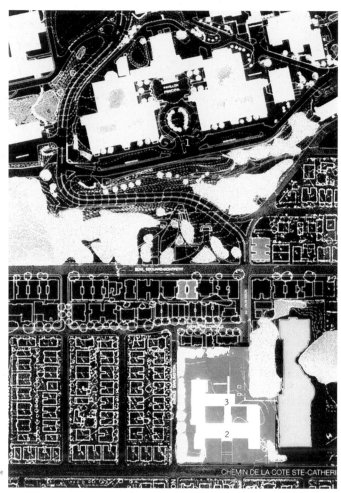

chemin de la Côte Ste-Catherine

site plan

0   5   10m

avenue Darlington

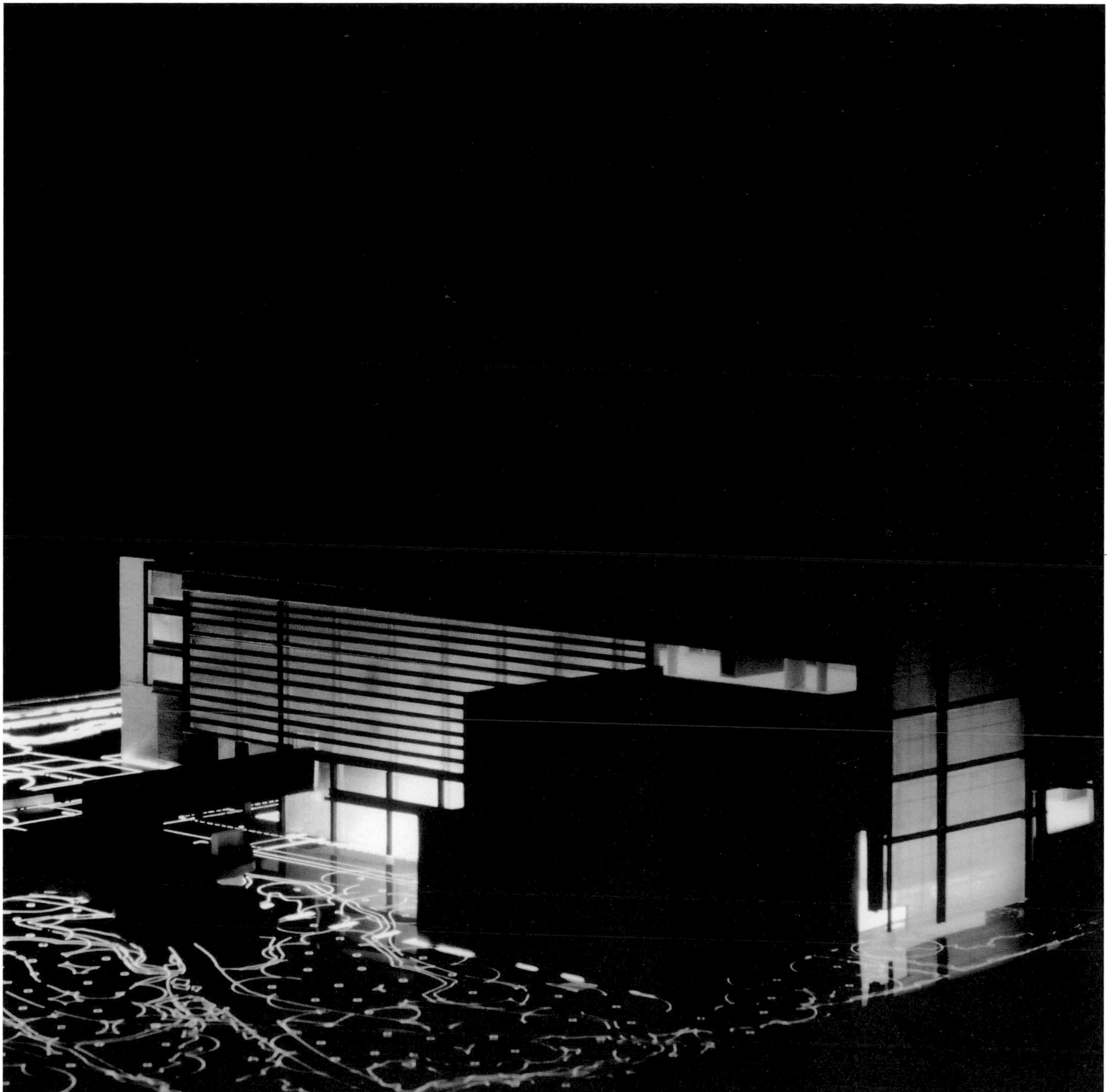

1 main entrance
2 hall
3 new auditorium
4 central circulation core
5 crltlque room
6 studios
7 faculty offices
8 courtyard with exhibition space below
9 library

second floor

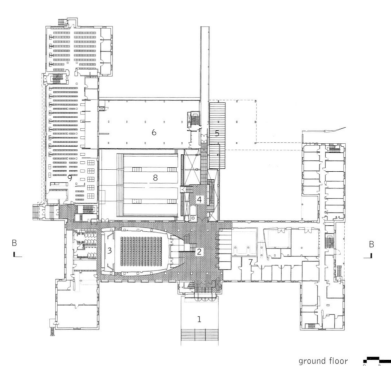

ground floor

0   5   10   20m

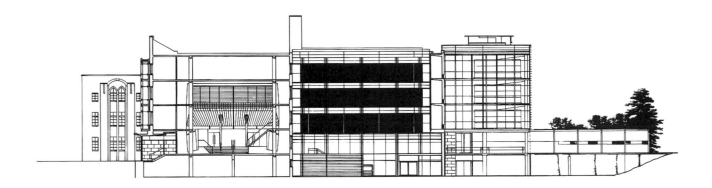

section A: through main hall and lower courtyard

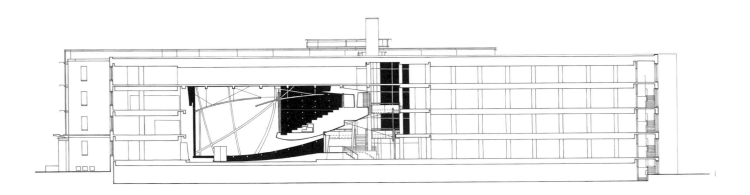

section B: through auditorium

0 1   5   10m

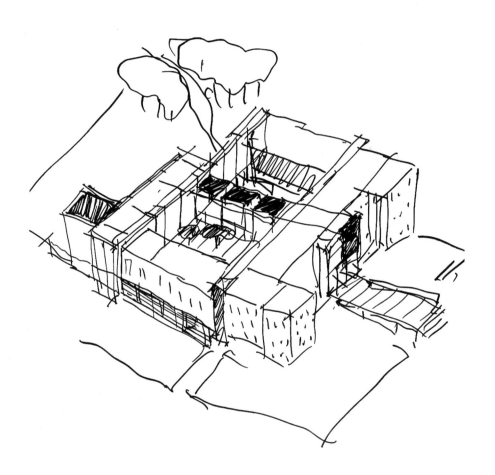

Museum of Video Arts and Exhibition Galleries | The character of the new Cinémathèque Québécoise

was established by both its site and program. Built in a slot of space between two existing structures, the main public functions of the Cinémathèque face inward to a courtyard. A connecting link across the back of the site houses a café, a small cinema and exhibition gallery. This connection also frames an outdoor dining terrace that is accessible from the street through the courtyard. | The main entrance is a "light box" facing Boulevard de Maisonneuve, which is connected to the street by a delicate steel bridge across a cut in the ground. As the word "light" refers to conditions of both weight and illumination, so the design of this particular box explores both of those qualities within the context of the moving image. The museum is signed by a gridded glass screen that projects out over the doors of the entry lobby and also extends beyond the box as a conspicuous layer drawn across the restored brick and stone facade of the old school building. A piece of this glazed skin is translucent and forms a screen onto which moving images are projected and can be viewed from the street. A ramped walkway through the public spaces of the Cinémathèque is located between projector and screen, creating silhouetted images of people moving within the building. | In sharp contrast to the widely assumed idea of the cinema as a sealed and introverted space, the light box and entry hall were developed to act also as a cinema. This space is available to visitors as they wait or wander through the galleries of the Cinémathèque. A screen suspended opposite the entrance lobby faces a balcony designed to seat 50 people. With views over the entrance hall and to this screen, the arrangement opens new relationships between observer and observed in ways that the traditional cinema rarely achieves, to give a new dimension to the experience and understanding of the "moving image." | The material palette of the foyer is subtly monochromatic, suggesting a fusion of transparency and the black and white of film. A series of glass and steel layers filter light and expose fragments of the concrete structure of the existing school. The building creates and frames a series of glimpses. Combining activity and artefact, old buildings and new, actor and audience, street and room, they are images that are projected into the life and spaces of the city. **Montréal 1997**

CINÉMATHÈQUE QUÉBÉCOISE

1   main entrance
2   existing Cinémathèque
3   new building
4   courtyard
5   School of Cinema

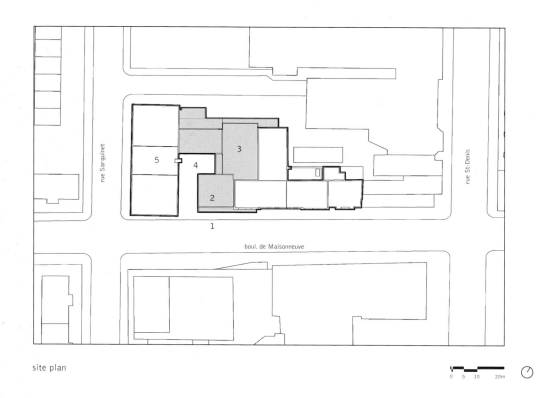

site plan

0   5   10   20m

1   main entrance

2   steel bridge

3   hall

4   projection booth / screen

5   balcony

6   exterior screen

7   156-seat cinema

8   86-seat cinema

9   ramped walkway

10 exhibition gallery

11 café

12 outdoor dining terrace

13 offices

14 School of Cinema

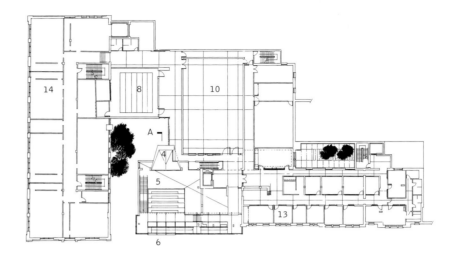

second floor

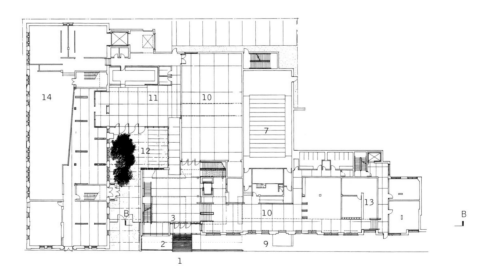

ground floor   0   5   10m

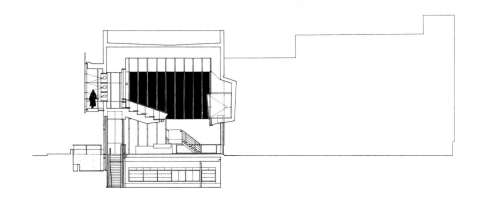

section A: through ramped walkway and balcony

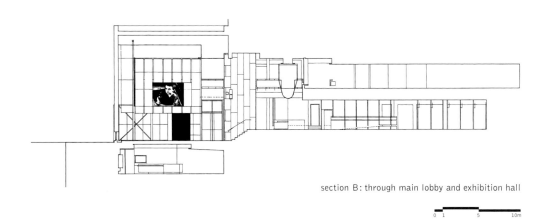

section B: through main lobby and exhibition hall

0 1   5   10m

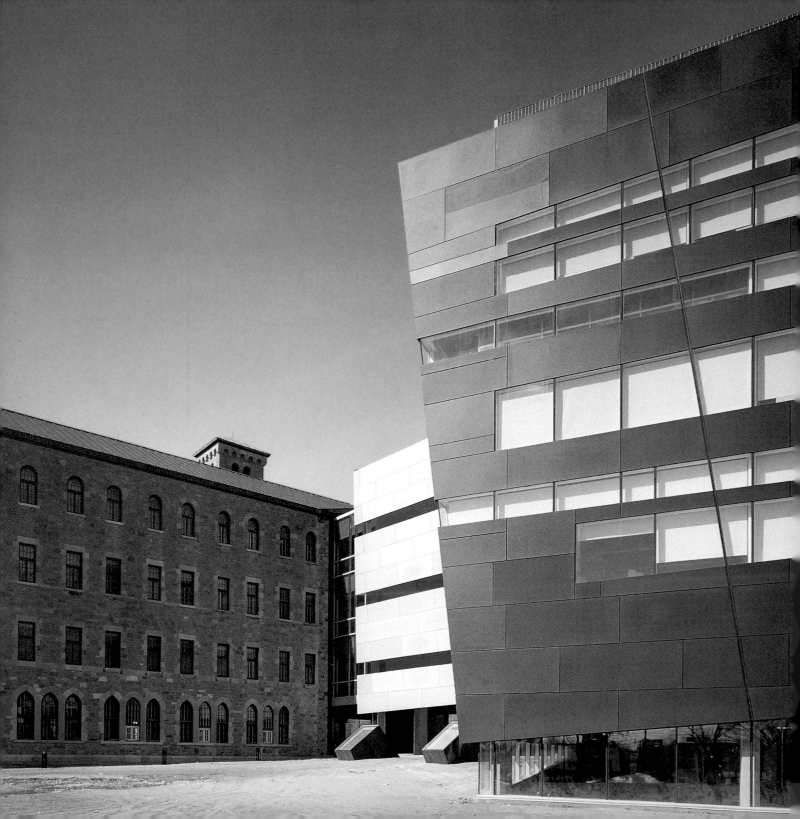

French College

French College | A former Jesuit monastery adjacent to the Rivière-des-Prairies has a commanding presence in the village of Sainte-Geneviève. The Lombard-style building, designed by architect Lucien Parent and built in 1933, was chosen to house a new French college at the western extremity of the island of Montréal. The existing building, built in concrete and wrapped with a local stone veneer, is situated on a small hill in 3.5 hectares of gently sloping landscape with a peninsula stretching north into the river. It has two lateral wings that define a covered cloister near the former bell tower. This most recent change of function necessitated a radical transformation of the existing structure as well as the addition of a new wing. The new program includes classrooms, laboratories, sports facilities, a library, offices for teachers and administration spaces, as well as a multi-functional theatre seating 350 that can be used by the public. | The conceptual strategy for developing the site recalls the origins of the French village while creating a fictitious archaeology for the site. A new axis is defined by a series of subterranean spaces that lie between the new and existing buildings. By locating the sports facility and theatre underground, the overall massing of the addition has been reduced and the site has been reoriented to the river. The theatre opens onto an exterior stage near the bank of the river. Two skylights jutting from the ground illuminate the foyer of the theatre and hint at the presence of an invisible subterranean world. | Classrooms and laboratories are housed in a sculpted block that is suspended over this excavated ground. The building is defined by a new taut external skin of black aluminum. The ground level cafeteria is the physical connection between the new archaeological landscape and the class-room and laboratory building above. Along the east-west axis that merges the new building with the college library in the former chapel, many of the existing walls of the monastery were removed to expand the interior spaces and connect them to the interior courtyard. **Montréal 2000**

COLLÈGE GÉRALD-GODIN

1   former monastery
2   cloister
3   new college
4   exterior passage

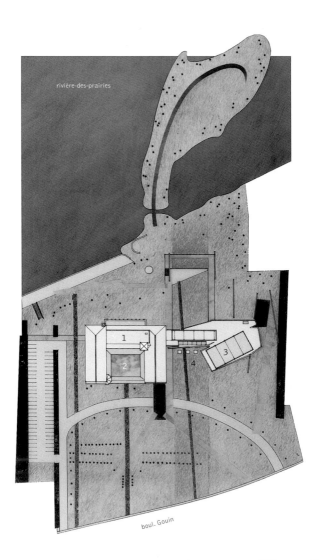

rivière-des-prairies

boul. Gouin

site plan

   0   10 20m

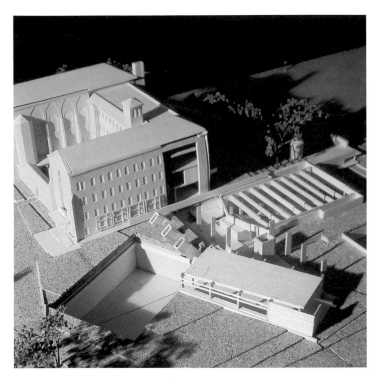
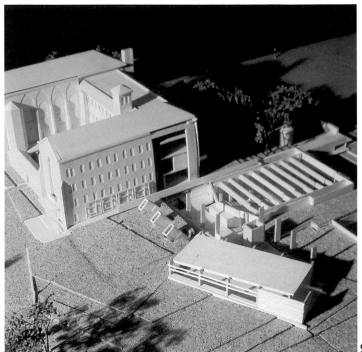

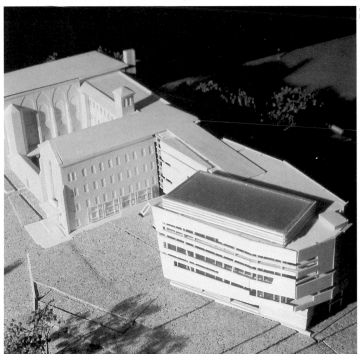

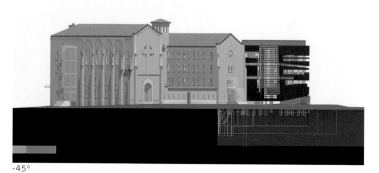

-45°

0°

45°

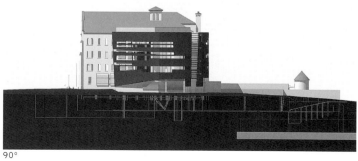

90°

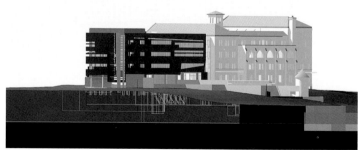

135°

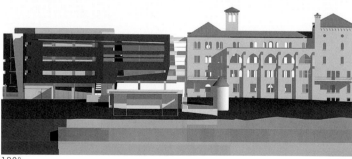

180°

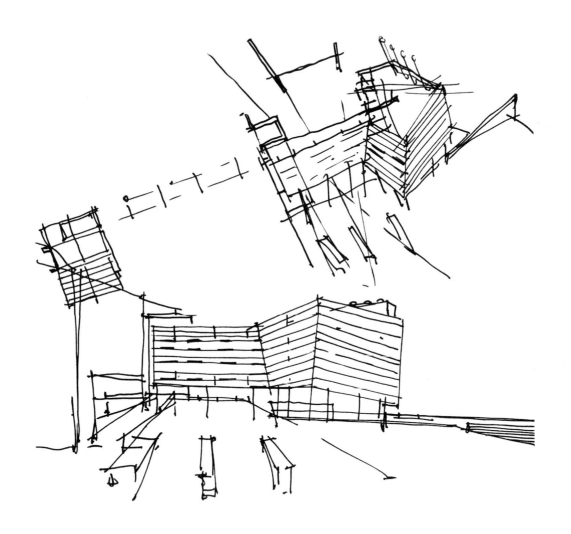

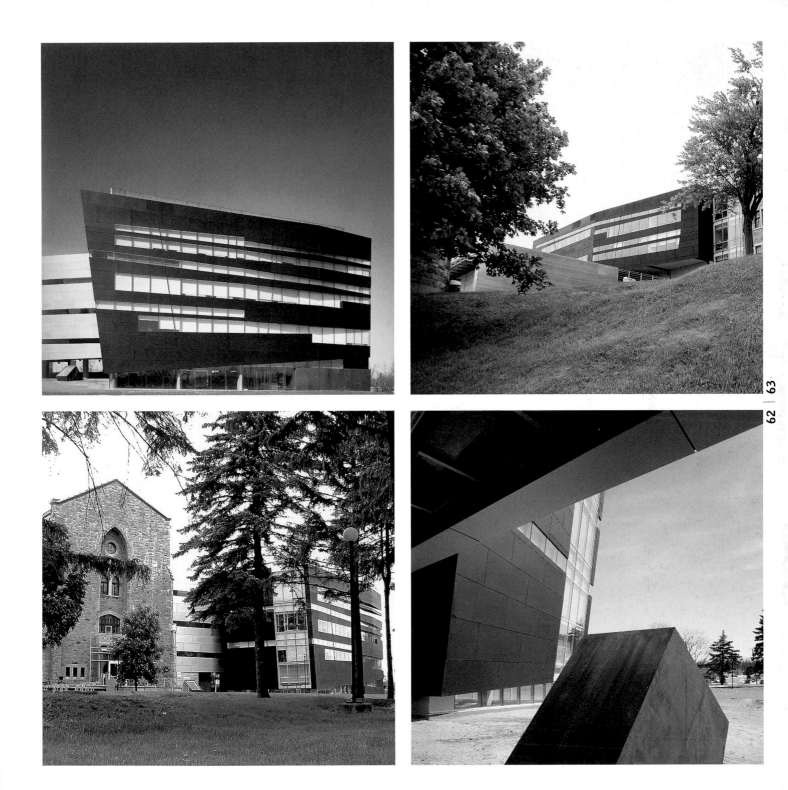

1 exterior passage
2 main entrance
3 belvedere
4 skylights
5 foyer
6 multifunctional theatre
7 cloister
8 library
9 offices
10 laboratories
11 cafeteria
12 agora
13 central link
14 classroom
15 gymnasium

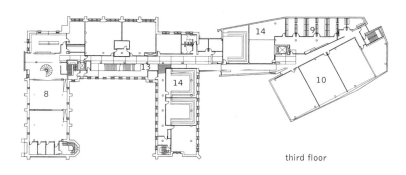

third floor

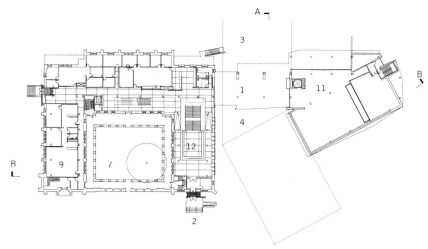

ground floor

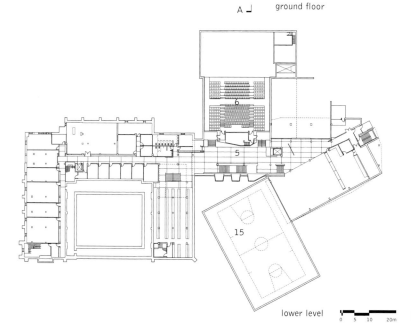

lower level

0   5   10   20m

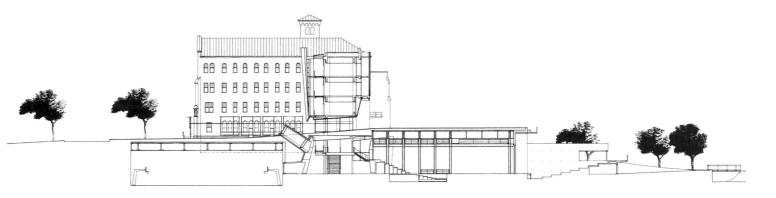

section A: through link, gymnasium and theatre

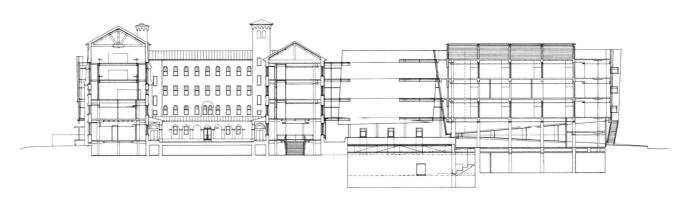

section B: through cloister and laboratories

01   5   10m

[2000 – 1997]

Montréal Pavilion, Shanghai — 2000

Salon Orbite – 1998

Salon Orbite – 1998

Radix – 1997

Montréal Pavilion

After years of cultural and commercial exchange between Shanghai and Montréal, the Mayor of Shanghai invited the Mayor of Montréal to build a pavilion in the Central Park of Pudong. To take advantage of this opportunity, the City of Montréal decided to build a pavilion that represents the technological reality of contemporary Canada and promotes Canadian enterprises, products and expertise in China. Situated in the centre of a 4-hectare garden within a 136-hectare park next to the new business centre of Shanghai, the pavilion was to foster commercial exchanges between the two countries. The concept consists of two indivisible elements: a ground inspired by the scale and power of the landscape that shaped Canadian culture, and an integrated high-tech pavilion. The building is a showcase that marks the presence of Canada in China. It is like a technological lantern embedded in the landscape of Shanghai. From the approach on the park's ceremonial road, the pavilion reads as a bridge to an island in a large pond. An exterior walkway crosses and separates two glass boxes on the bridge. These luminous exhibition halls reflect on the surface of the water, while offices, a boutique and permanent exhibition spaces have been cut into a hill and rendered invisible. The main exhibition spaces are conceived as virtual gardens, with large projection screens where images of the Canadian landscape alternate with promotional images of the country's latest technologies. The transparency of the pavilion creates a dialogue between these images and the environment of the park. Special attention was given to making the building environmentally responsible. This has prompted the creation of a new landscape based on the use of natural flora. In addition, the main building is partially buried underground so as to reduce the pavilion's visual impact in the park and water from the lake is used for cooling in the air circulation system. The pavilion, which also houses an electrical substation for the city, is configured as a bridge between two banks, and the walkway remains open throughout the day and night to maintain pedestrian circulation through the park. **Shanghai 2000**

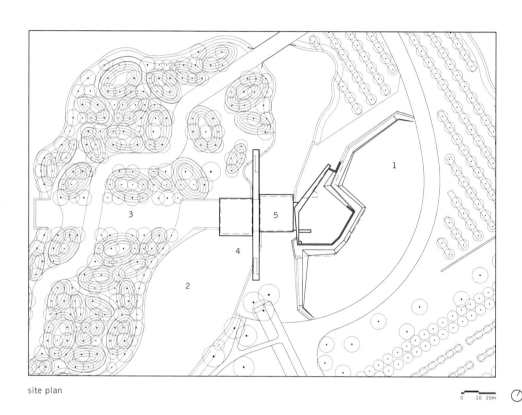

1 interior exhibition
2 exterior exhibition
3 lanterns
4 boutique

site plan

0 10 20m

1 ceremonial road
2 lake
3 island
4 exterior bridge
5 pavilion

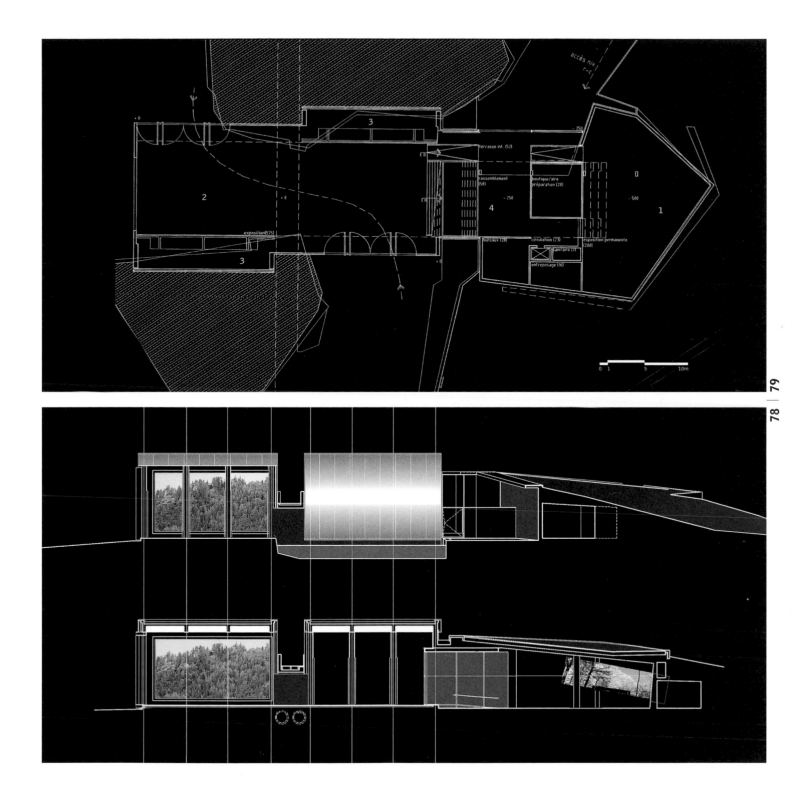

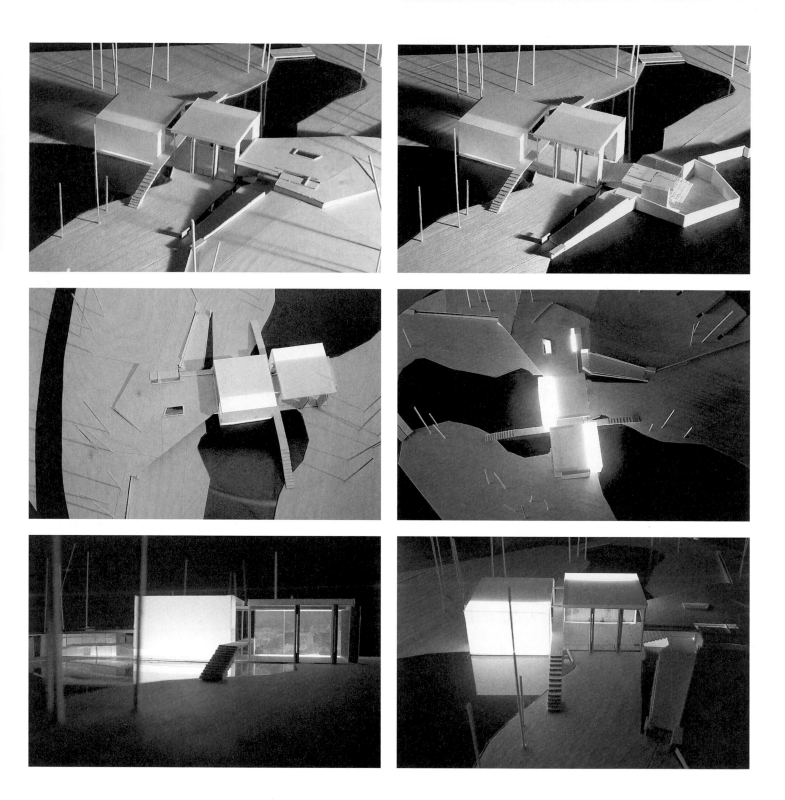

First Nations Garden Pavilion

The First Nations Garden is a permanent commemoration of the great peace of Montréal of 1701. It is a crossroads of cultures, designed to help visitors discover the culture of the first inhabitants of North America. It also offers an opportunity for the First Nations to share their traditions, wisdom and knowledge. | The pavilion is a museum within a garden. Sheltering less than 2% of the garden grounds, the pavilion is mostly outdoor space. Built along the garden's main pathway, the pavilion metaphorically raises the path to reveal the cultural memory of the place. The undulating roof recalls a wisp of smoke through the trees. Outdoor displays sheltered by the roof are framed by two indoor spaces at opposite ends of the pavilion: exhibition and orientation spaces at one end, public washrooms and a meeting space at the other. The pavilion also houses a boutique and offices. The relationship between building and site and the environmental sensitivity needed to maintain the spirit of the garden were critical to the design of the pavilion. The new building acts as both a filter and a link between two garden environments: an area of spruces and a maple forest. Wherever possible, the pavilion's exhibitions are planned outdoors. These exterior spaces orient the visitor and help reduce the apparent size of the building by integrating the exhibition with the wider environment. Vertical surfaces are minimized to limit the visual impact of the building on the environment, and half of the built spaces are located underground to further reduce the influence of the building on its setting. The new building was sited to retain existing trees and maintain a relatively open terrain in an attempt to integrate the building with the site. In addition, the selection of materials — poured-in-place concrete, wood and weathering steel — helps ground the pavilion in the landscape. **Montréal 2000**

JARDIN BOTANIQUE

1　lake

2　evergreen forest

3　deciduous forest

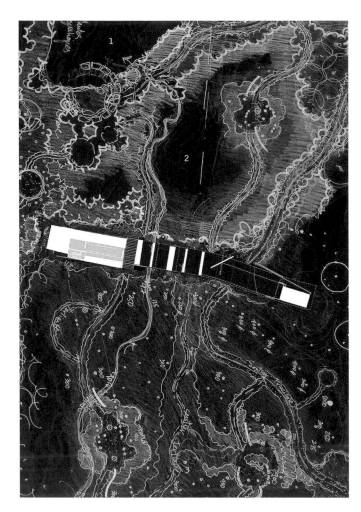

site plan

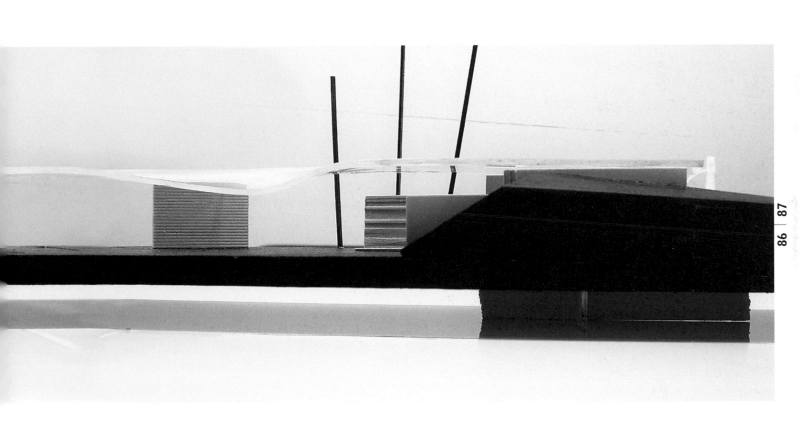

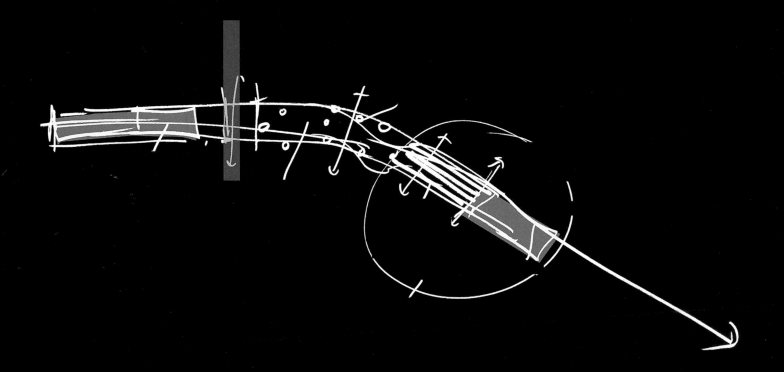

1 exterior exhibition area
2 interior exhibition area
3 offices
4 boutique
5 restrooms
6 ramp to lower level

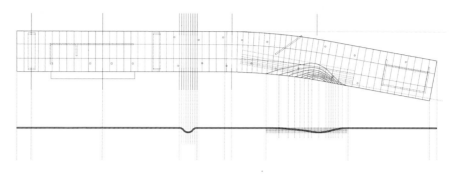

roof, plan and section

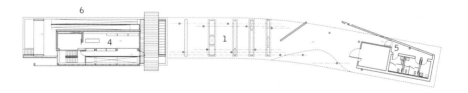

ground floor

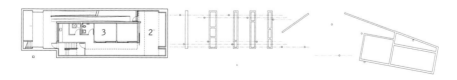

lower level

0 1   5   10m

Faculty of Music | The design for the new Faculty of Music gives prominence to the southeastern corner of the

McGill University campus in the centre of Montréal. The new building is adjacent to the Strathcona Building, which houses one of the university's main concert facilities and is the current home of the Faculty of Music. The new program adds to the faculty space and includes a library, recital hall, state-of-the-art multimedia and practice studios, and faculty offices. | The site is a narrow strip of land on Rue Sherbrooke between Rue Aylmer and the east wing of the existing faculty. The design is anchored by a multimedia studio: a polished limestone volume, almost five storeys high, that is embedded three storeys into the ground at the north end of the site. Practice rooms and technical studios are also located underground, south of the multimedia studio. The recital hall and main entrance are above, at street level. A folded concrete plane defines these spaces and appears to support the main body of the building above. This plane evokes an eroded ground plane that leads to Mont Royal beyond. A three-storey library sits immediately above the recital hall, with three storeys of office and practice space above the library. The new building is linked to the rest of the faculty by a glazed bridge that runs through the main entrance hall. | The building's east and west façades are discrete planes that frame views of the city along Rue Aylmer. Each façade is patterned to evoke musical figures. The east façade has been designed in black and grey zinc, with long strip windows that light the office corridors, and a large glazed opening into the library entry space. The west façade is a pattern of matte and polished aluminum that reflects the Strathcona Building while a series of punched windows bring light into the smaller spaces inside. **Montréal 2000**

McGILL UNIVERSITY

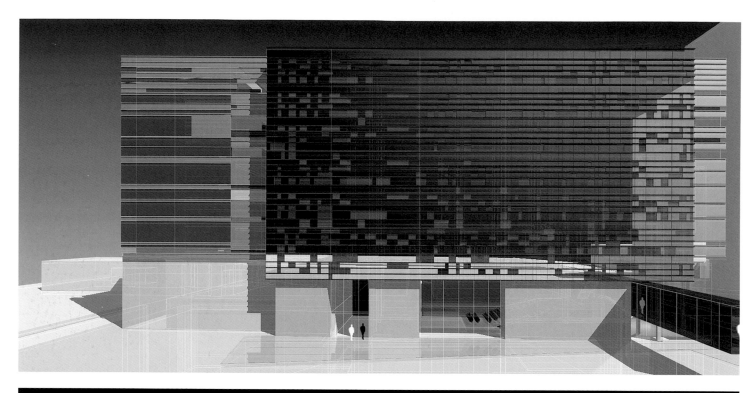

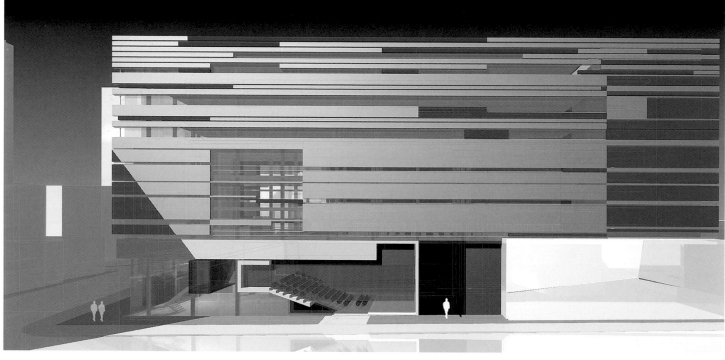

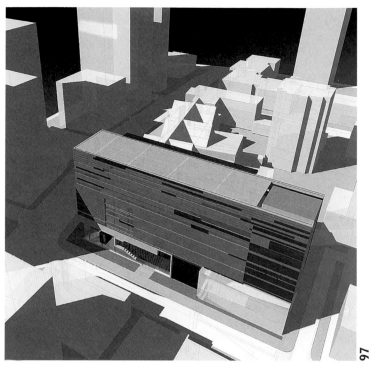

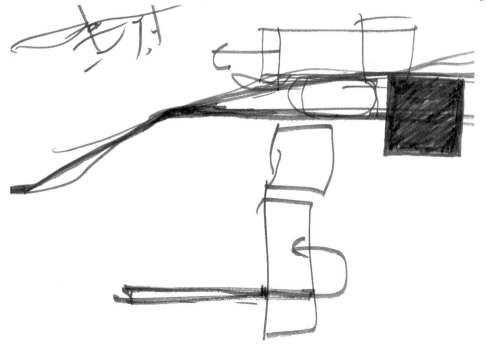

[1997 – 1989]

Cinémathèque Québécoise – 1997

Université de Montréal – 1996

Résidence Mercille – 1993

Cossette Communications – 1995

Blitz   Cossette   Geyser   Graphème   Impact Recherche   Optimum

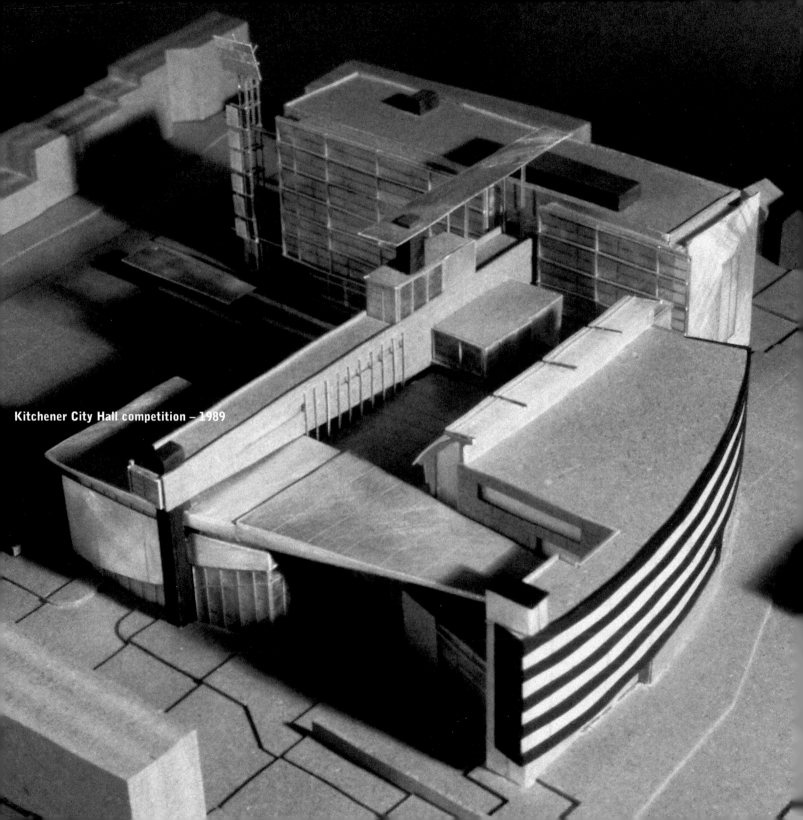

Kitchener City Hall competition — 1989

Theatre | The design for the new Théâtre Bordée maintains the spirit and expression of the existing theatre and the historic neighbourhood of St. Rock, in Québec. The main volumes and structural axes are drawn from the old theatre, and in this way the design respects the history of the building and reinforces the presence of the original façade. Re-using the fly-tower and rotating the theatre ninety degrees, parallel to Rue St- Joseph, emphasizes the main hall. The vertically organized theatre brings the audience close to the stage and separates the foyer and balcony access. The existing main façade and lateral wall are retained and front the administrative functions. | Each element of the program is discretely expressed and separated by glazing. A glass partition wall reveals the slope of the main seating level in the hall while a glass skin under the existing façade exposes the interior spaces: major circulation corridors, bar, stair to the balcony, offices and rehearsal hall. These are differentiated through light and with the use of colour: intense saturated colour for the balcony, and natural light that is controlled by mobile panels in the rehearsal hall. These colours fall on one transforming surface of glass that is translucent above to shield the practice spaces and transparent below to open up the public spaces. | A café has been planned below the main hall and is directly accessible from the street; however, patrons are always in visual contact with the form and activity of the theatre. The administrative offices animate the Rue St-Joseph frontage both day and night. Above the complex, the rehearsal space receives natural light and gives access to a covered terrace on top of the old theatre. The two studios and administration offices also have access to this protected private space, with a view of the surrounding neighbourhood. **Québec 2000**

LA BORDÉE

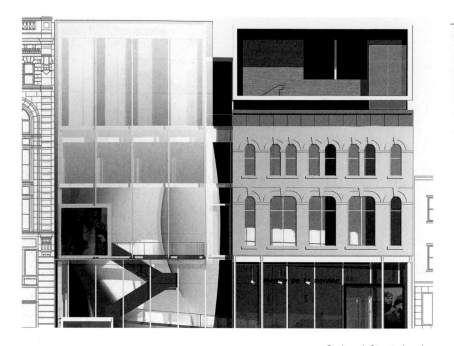

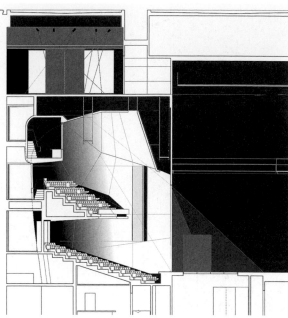

St-Joseph Street elevation

section through theatre showing rehearsal spaces above

1 main hall
2 stair to café
3 foyer
4 stage – fly tower
5 balcony

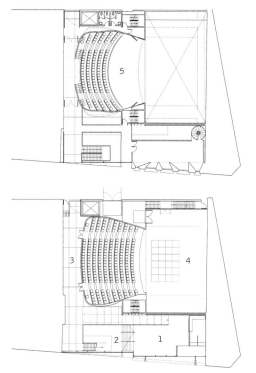

balcony level

0   5   10m

ground floor

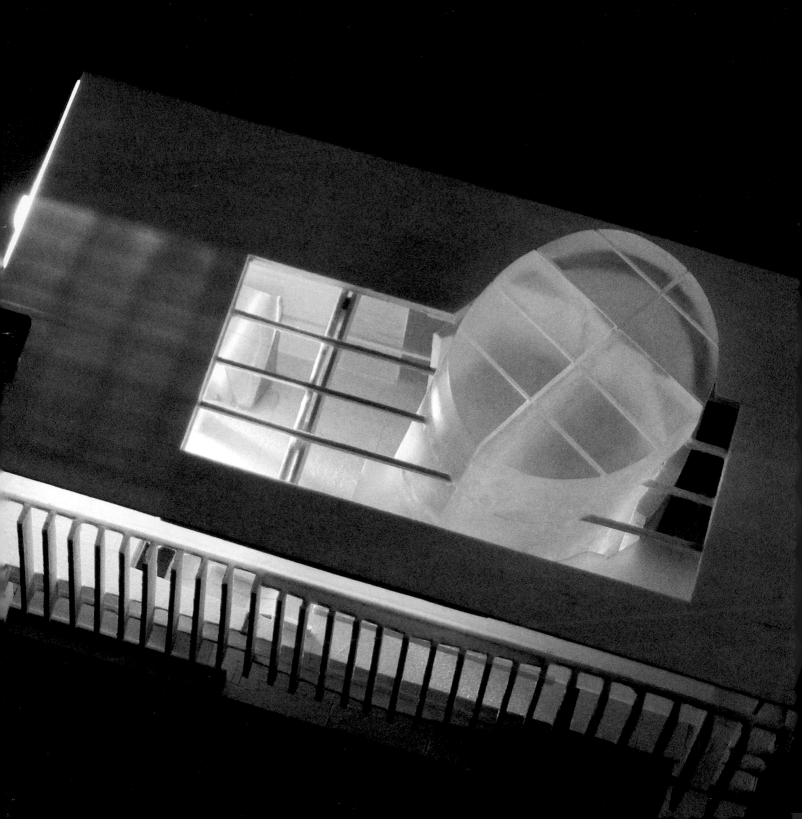

Music and Arts Centre | This project, in the centre of the town of Jyväskylä, Finland, was designed to utilize the spaces of the Defence Corps Building designed by Alvar Aalto, which houses the art museum. The new building contains concert hall facilities, including chamber music and rehearsal halls. The design of this project explores the perception and continuity of space. The vertical and horizontal axes of circulation serve as references against which the building is experienced. | The composition of light and colour is critical. A series of solid blades separated by glass sheets forms a facade that would screen the interior from the city. This wall extends the length of Vapaudenkatu to define the main public space within. The parallax created by the changing rhythm of the blades alternately exposes and conceals the exterior landscape, depending on movement and location. From a distance this screen, although static, gives the impression of a subtle dimensional transformation. It is animated by the movement of people. This transformation is also accentuated by opposing colour treatments on the sides of the blades. The black of one side gives a slowly vanishing, undulating rhythm, whereas the opposing white assimilates the skin of the building with the white volume of the concert hall. Moving past the punctuated blades at close range creates a staccato series of sharp, clear visual images, experienced as one moves either along the street outside or towards the concert hall inside. The last blade on Kilpisenkatu is stretched to form a translucent façade facing the park, obscuring the interior activity of the complex. | The functions of the building are separated into discrete formal elements and are arranged loosely on the concrete floor plates. These plates are visible from the public hall, and the open space between these elements orients the visitor to the larger volume. A double envelope of glass wraps the cylindrical concert hall and is visible from all points within the complex. Lit from within, this envelope evokes a massive, striated block cut from glacial ice. The acoustics of the hall are controlled by an integrated system of sliding curtains that move horizontally around the circular rings of the volume. The form of the concert hall is reduced at the upper levels to create a sense of intimacy. **Finland 1998**

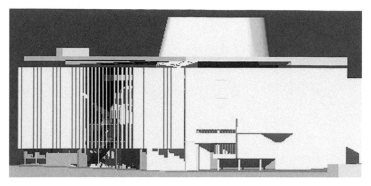
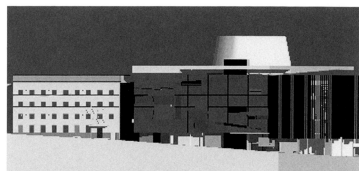

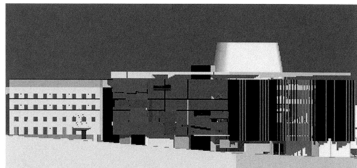
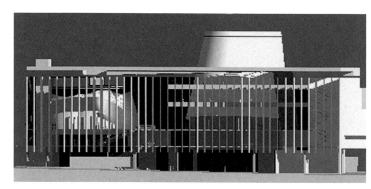
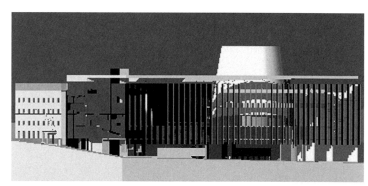
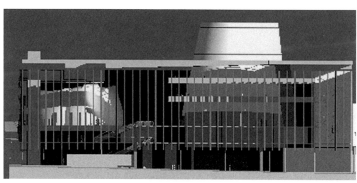

1 stair to main foyer
2 café
3 foyer
4 concert hall
5 multifunctional theatre
6 exhibition space
7 services

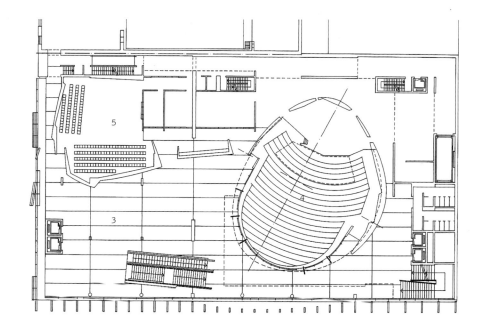

foyer level

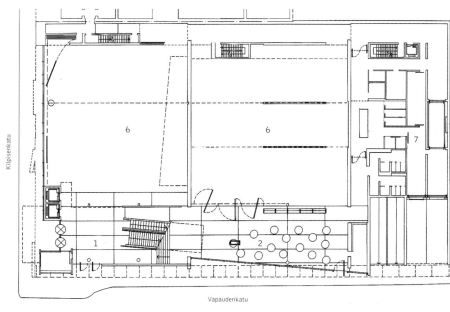

ground floor

0 1   5   10m

Canadian Embassy

The design proposal for the Canadian Embassy in Berlin was developed to reflect the openness of Canadian society and represent the beauty of its natural landscape. The project was designed for an urban site in the heart of Berlin. Located on a corner fronting Leipziger Platz, the building opens at grade in an attempt to make the public functions of the embassy visible. The design of the main façade was developed as a 14m thick carved solid. It contains activities that support cultural exchange and provides views into and out of a newly created inner garden courtyard. This courtyard also provides access to the different activities planned for the building: office, retail and residential spaces. The commercial space has been planned on several floors on the north side of the courtyard with frontage on both Ebertstrasse and Vosstrasse. A series of residential units front onto Ebertstrasse, Vosstrasse and Leipziger Platz where they have good views and gain natural ventilation. | The ground plane of the courtyard consists of sculpted plates of stone that connect the two sides of the site. The garden courtyard has been designed to represent four symbolic elements of the Canadian landscape: water, rock, plain and forest. These abstracted gardens serve as a memory of the landscape that molded Canadian culture and they are the heart of the embassy. Three of these elements – rock, plain and water – are within the ground plane that leads the visitor through the court into the embassy reception level. The forest defines the embassy reception space and extends up through the full height of the building, connecting the reception areas on all floors. | Aligned with the structural grid, a glass lens extends upward from the sculpted ground. Both reflective and transparent, this is the essential line of security between the public and private spaces of the embassy. It also defines the principle linear circulation route at each floor. Primary public functions are located on one side, allowing access from the open courtyard or controlled access through the embassy. The embassy spaces that require security are distributed to the west and south of the courtyard, between floors one and five. Security is zoned vertically, with the most public functions at the lower levels. In addition, each floor has been designed to permit growth and change within the embassy without compromising security. **Berlin 1999**

LEIPZIGER PLATZ

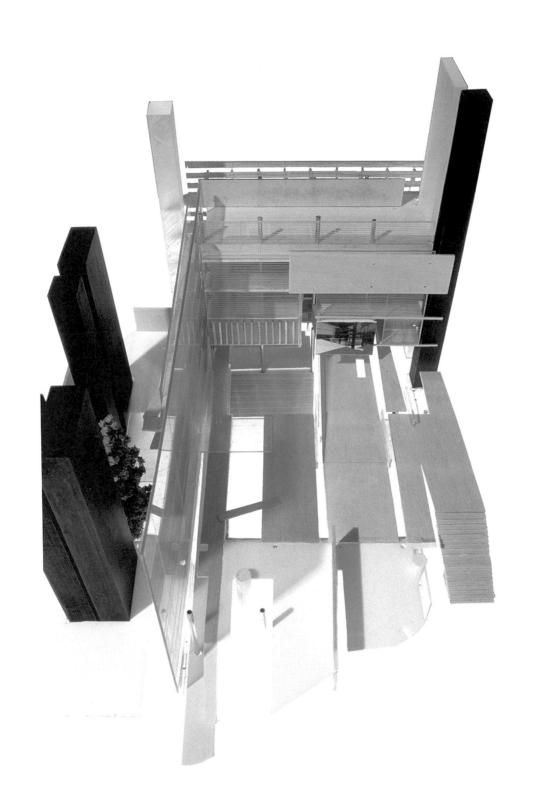

1 exhibition space

2 ground plane / reception level

3 interior garden

4 offices

5 retail / commercial

6 agora

7 gallery

8 restricted area

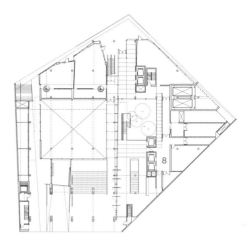

ground floor

lower level

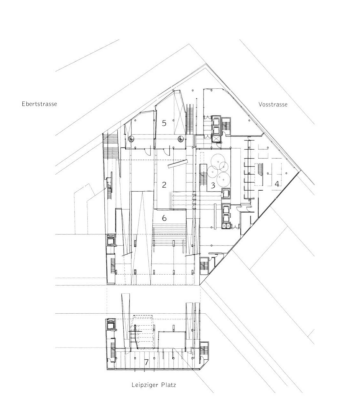

main level and mezzanine level

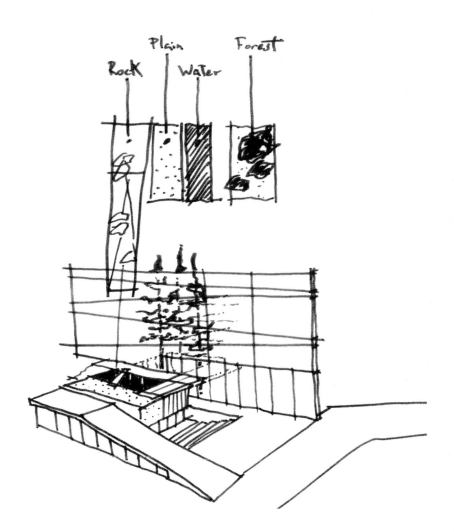

Rock Plain Water Forest

Library | The design for the Grande Bibliothèque du Québec recalls the gentle topography surrounding Mont Royal. The building has been planned on seven levels within the envelope of a long, rectangular box bounded by four existing streets. The main entry sequence follows the gentle slope of the site toward the main reception area of the library that is located under a luminous hanging exterior garden. This garden of vibrant natural light marks the presence of the Québec Collection, housed in a glass object illuminated from within. All the library's controlled activities are located in this zone of coloured light. From the reception area, visitors move obliquely toward the Québec Collection and the gardens at the level of Rue Sherbrooke. A series of interior and exterior gardens define the crest of a virtual hill, created by oblique partitions of transparent glass. | The long north-south axis defines the spirit of the building's two main façades. The context of each is different, and this difference has influenced their design. The façade on Rue Berri recalls the speed of the city. It accompanies the ascending and descending motion of visitors on the building's escalators and walkways, and its surface is like a snapshot of the luminous traces that moving cars leave on photographic film. The series of long horizontal metal bands, some undulating, respond to this ever-moving coloured light. By contrast, the façade on Avenue Savoie, a quiet street, contains most of the reading areas. Oriented west, it offers views to the city. This inhabitable façade is a refuge, a place for reflection. Its long translucent glass surface becomes increasingly transparent toward the centre and reveals the exterior garden, also visible from Rue St-Denis. Variation in transparency gives the illusion of a long, curved surface punctuated by a series of small colourful gardens. The Québec Collection receives natural light from the interior garden. From this point, all the major spaces of the entrance hall are visible and accessible. The Québec Collection also opens onto the exterior garden to create a space that has been designed for special events in good weather. | Formal and material references to Montréal's indigenous landscape define the spirit of the new library. Circulation paths and the surfaces in public spaces relate to local materials and plants. Three zones of planting follow the north-south axis of the square, the interior and exterior gardens, and the courtyard. Birches, planted with an increasing density, extend from a sparse plantation in the square to the dense forest in the courtyard. **Montréal 2001**

GRANDE BIBLIOTHÈQUE DU QUÉBEC

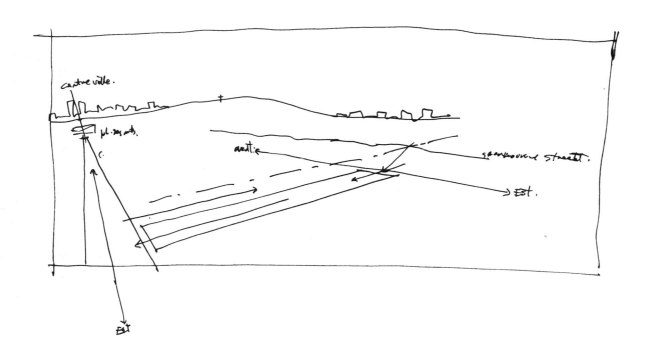

centre ville.

pl. des arts.

c.

arctic

grandmaouvre straalt.

→ Est.

Est

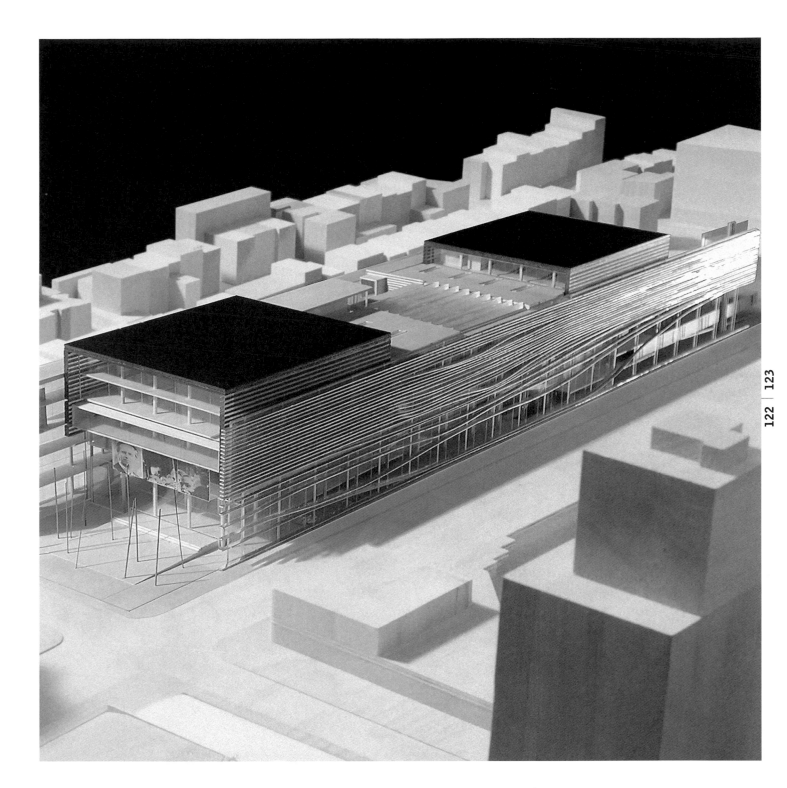

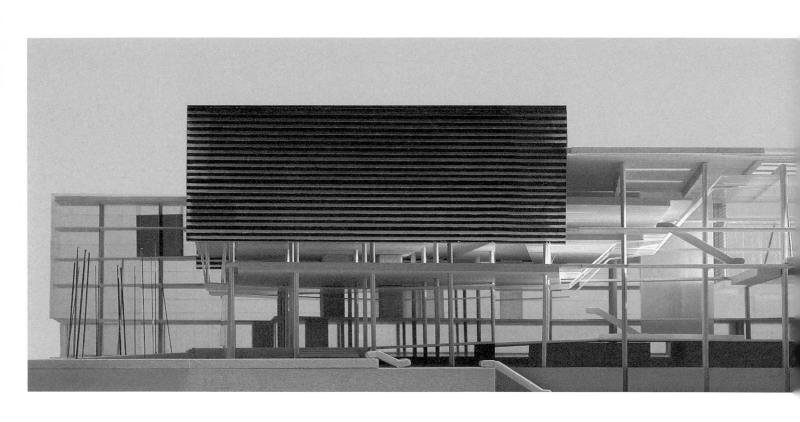

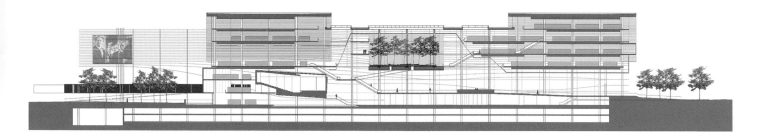

section A

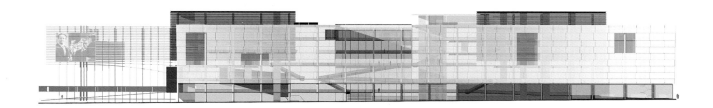

avenue Savoie elevation

0   10   20m

1 reception area
2 Québec Collection
3 reading areas
4 interior garden
5 exterior garden
6 children's area

second floor plan

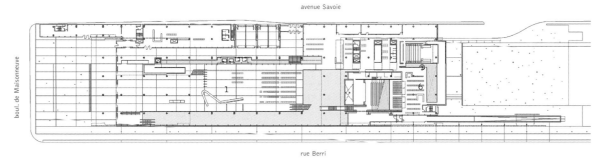

ground floor plan

0   10   20m

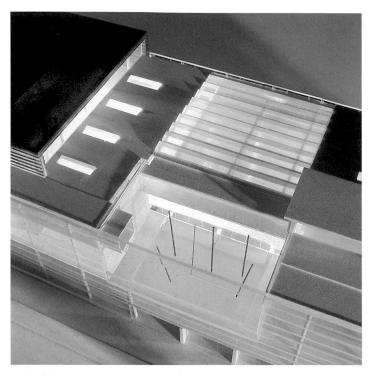

University Complex | This proposal for an academic building in Montréal is organized around a new internal public space that is parallel to Rue Ste-Catherine. The Faculty of Engineering and Computer Science above completes the continuity of the street. | On the west side of Rue Guy, a pavilion housing the department of Commerce and Administration is located behind a glazed façade that creates the fourth face of an urban complex defined by the existing GM building to the north. A vibrant and luminous volume located in the heart of this new complex houses the Faculty of Fine Arts and Visual Arts. | This new integrated complex introduces a critical mass to the heart of the Sir George Williams Campus. The development responds to the existing urban setting and projects a progressive image of Concordia University. | All interior passages converge on a new internal "folded garden." Positioned parallel to student activities, this garden and the commercial and exhibition spaces alongside are open to the public. | From Rue Ste-Catherine a series of steps, anchored by vertical circulation cores, direct the visitor to the "folded garden" beyond. This large gathering space common to all faculties is defined by a surface that will be translucent by day and luminous at night. It folds around the auditorium, the foyer and the garden like a ribbon. It also becomes the link between the various elements of the program, and an orienting element for the visitor. Escalators connect the garden to the first floor level and permit the efficient movement of students and staff at peak hours. | The integrated complex also provides pedestrian access to Guy metro station and direct access to the existing sports centre that is located on the lower levels of the Commerce and Administration building. | A sense of openness and accessibility is accentuated throughout the new complex, which reflects a desire to communicate and to welcome. The new pavilions are very permeable at street level and are envisaged as becoming focal points for the student community. This transparency is also meant to exhibit the technologies that underlie the evolution of the knowledge base of the university. | The exterior treatment of the new pavilions evokes an image of modernity that reflects Concordia's progress, celebrated recently in its 25th anniversary. It also establishes an architectural language that is coherent throughout each phase, while giving each faculty its own distinct identity. **Montréal 2001**

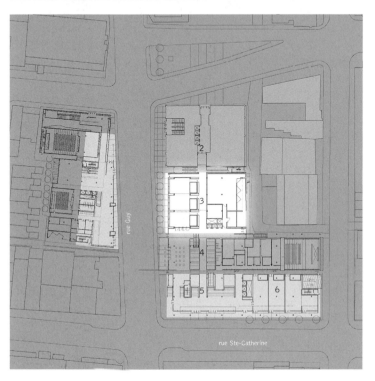

1 Commerce and Administration pavilion
2 GM building
3 Faculty of Fine Arts and Visual Arts
4 folded garden
5 Faculty of Engineering and Computer Science
6 commercial spaces

Paysage et sensation

Armés du seul désir ardent de construire, Gilles Saucier et André Perrotte se sont frayé un chemin créatif unique dans le milieu culturel de l'architecture canadienne, remontant le fleuve, en parcourant ses rives, nourris de la simple beauté des paysages où la terre, l'eau et le ciel se rencontrent dans un horizon lumineux et coloré toujours surprenant et sur lequel se greffent villages et villes, signes humains, architectures habitées, lieux incandescents où l'expérience du monde est à la mesure de son immensité. En suivant leur démarche, volontaire, investigatrice et gourmande, on constate l'évidence de cette préoccupation pour l'instabilité de l'horizon, le plaisir d'exister, qui se traduit par un équilibre toujours étudié entre l'abstraction et la matérialité, le volume et la surface, le visuel et le tactile, l'intériorité et l'extériorité : une orchestration subtile de la logique des sensations et des formes. Il n'y a pas chez eux de lourds arguments réthoriques, de manifestes combatifs, d'exhibitions savantes d'un parcours réflexif ardu. Leurs œuvres se forgent dans la modernité assumée, avec les outils du moment, en s'appuyant sur ses propres sources projectives. Cet a priori sur la beauté du monde et sur le sentiment que nous habitons un paysage, définit une attitude éthique où le dessin porte le regard, les détails constructifs expriment l'idée, l'espace réalisé installe le lieu. L'architecture de Gilles Saucier et d'André Perrotte peut être vue comme une forme paysagère (landform) au sens où l'entend Kenneth Frampton.

Dans ce cas, nous pourrions souligner qu'il s'agit d'une forme paysagère critique, c'est-à-dire une forme architecturale qui refuse «le paysagisme», la fusion ou l'indétermination entre le site et la construction. Ce qu'ils nous proposent, c'est plutôt une subtile différenciation, une imbrication des sols, un dédoublement de l'horizon, une expérience toujours renouvelée des rencontres de la terre, de l'eau et du ciel. Cette disposition créative s'affirme dès les premiers projets et, par la suite, dans les réalisations les plus modestes autant que dans les plus importantes par leur caractère institutionnel. Les «possibles» y sont mesurés, jamais transposés, toujours réinventés comme si un thème ordonnait la composition toujours claire, les matières qui sonnent justes, le dessin ferme et précis. Le projet est donc transportable. Il est une sorte d'embarcation. Ainsi, on ne peut se contenter du déjà-là, de quelque génie du lieu, ou de ces bizzareries de la pensée qui voudraient que l'homme soit immobile, sur place, pour toujours. Il n'y a pas de nostalgie bricolée qui se ferait mémoire de circonstance. Ce mouvement, c'est une façon de voir autrement, de comprendre ce continent, de prendre amoureusement ce territoire, comme un morceau du monde qui n'attendait que nous pour être redécouvert. Gilles Saucier et André Perrotte transcrivent méticuleusement, pour notre seul plaisir, leurs passages vers de nouveaux horizons. Comme le poète Arthur Rimbaud, chacun d'eux peut dire : «Et j'ai vu quelquefois ce que l'homme a cru voir» et nous en faire partager l'expérience étonnante dans leurs réalisations architecturales.

Armed only with a burning desire to build, Gilles Saucier and André Perrotte have carved out a uniquely creative path in the cultural world of Canadian architecture. They have been nourished by the simple beauty of Canada's landscapes, where earth, water and sky meet at a luminous, coloured, ever astonishing horizon, and inspired by towns and villages, human signs, occupied dwellings and incandescent places where earthly experience is equal to the vastness of the world. In tracing their voyage, one sees evidence of a concern with the instability of the horizon and the joy of living; this translates into a perpetually studied balance between abstraction and materialism, volume and surface, the visual and the tactile, the interior and the exterior: a subtle orchestration of the logic of feelings and forms. For them, there are no weighty rhetorical arguments, no combative manifestos, no scholarly displays of reflective and arduous thought. Their works are shaped by an embraced modernism. This 'a priori' view of the beauty of the world and of the sense that we inhabit a landscape which defines an ethical attitude where the design carries the vision, the construction details express the idea and the finished space anchors the place. The architecture of Gilles Saucier and André Perrotte might be viewed as landform in the sense of the word as used by Kenneth Frampton.

But in this case it is a critical landform, a style of architecture that rejects "excessive gardens," and the merging and indeterminate blending of site and building. What is proposed here is more of a subtle differentiation, a layering of the ground, a doubling of the horizon, a continuous renewal of the experience of earth, water and sky meeting. This creative tendency surfaced in their earliest endeavours and, subsequently, has continued to be reflected in all their projects - from the most modest to the grandest institutional works. The "possible" is always measured, never transposed, always re-invented. It is as if a theme were dictating that the composition must always be clear, the materials always ring true, the design always be firm and precise. The project is thus transportable - a kind of boat. One can never, therefore, be content with what is already there, with a kind of 'genius loci,' with those strange vagaries of the mind that would wish man to be immobile, locked in one place forever. This movement is another way of seeing, of understanding a continent, of lovingly embracing that territory. Gilles Saucier and André Perrotte meticulously transcribed their passages toward new horizons strictly for our pleasure. Like the poet Arthur Rimbaud, each could declare, "And sometimes I have seen what men have imagined they saw!" and invite us to share in the amazing experience of their architectural achievements.

Georges Adamczyk

Biography

Gilles Saucier (b. 1958) and André Perrotte (b. 1959) met while studying architecture in Québec. After graduating in 1982 they both worked in practice in Montréal. Between 1983 and 1988 Gilles Saucier worked for Saia and Cayouette Architects while André Perrotte worked at Bobrow and Fieldman and later with Poirier Cardinal Architects.

Since graduating they have both taught at UQAM School of Design in Montréal. Gilles Saucier has also taught in the School of Architecture at the Université de Montréal. He has been an invited critic and guest lecturer at several Canadian and U.S. universities, including Dalhousie University, University of Toronto, University of Michigan, New York Architectural League, University of Detroit, Washington University and SUNY Buffalo. In 2000 Gilles Saucier was made a Fellow of the Royal Architectural Institute of Canada.

Gilles Saucier and André Perrotte founded their own practice in Montréal in 1988. Their approach to design is research based and seeks spatial simplicity through the systematic exploration of intrinsic physical and poetic qualities of materials. Early interests in scenography and architecture have evolved to embrace the consideration of natural and urban landscapes. Saucier + Perrotte has offices in Montréal and Toronto.

The work of Saucier + Perrotte has received over thirty awards for design, including Governor General's Medals, Canadian Architect Awards, PA awards and OAQ awards of excellence. Since 1988, they have also been invited to participate in numerous design competitions. They were the winners of the Faculty of Design competition and finalists in the national competition to design a new Canadian Embassy in Berlin. The work of Saucier + Perrotte has been published internationally, appearing in Architectural Review, Architecture, Architectural Record, Canadian Architect, Abitare and Baumeister. It has also been exhibited widely, notably in 2000 in the Sottsass Room Series at the Canadian Centre for Architecture.

Team 1988 – 2002

Amale Andreos
Audrey Archambault
Aliye Eda Ascioglu
Thomas Balaban
Patrice Bégin
Anna Bendix
Andrew Butler
Natacha Bernèche
Guylaine Biron
Adrian Blackwell
Martin Bouchard
Yves Bouchard
Ewan Branda
Benoit Carrier
Nathalie Cloutier
Mathilde S Brisson
Eric Champagne
Jean-Michel Colonnier
Pierre Colpron
Trevor Davies
Alain Desforges
Darrell deGrandmont
Dominique Dumais
Robert D'Errico
Isabelle Dufour
Andrew Dunbar
Éric Dupras
Louis-Philippe Frappier
Maxime-Alexis Frappier
Maxime Gagné
Michel Gamache
Gail Greenberg
Olivier Grenier
Christian Hébert
Jean-Sébastien Herr
Bechara Hélal
Marie-Claude Hurtubise
Oscar Juarros
Anick Labrie
Lise Lachance
Julie Lafrenière
Jean-François Lagacé
Louis-Charles Lasnier
Martin Leblanc
Jean-Louis Léger
Laurence Le Beux
Yves Legris
Éric Majer
Laurence Marasti
Jean-François Mathieu
Deborah Mesher
Sergio Morales
Jean-Olivier Nadeau
Thanh Liem Nguyen
Claudio Nunez
Quinlan Osborne
Jean Pellan
Marc-André Plourde
Pierre-Alexandre Rhéaume
Benjamin Rankin
Joan Renaud
Guillaume Sasseville
Denise Saucier
Annie-Claude Sauvé
Sudhir Suri
Samantha Schneider
Pascale Tétrault
Franck Thonon
Guy Trudel

Project credits

Usine C - Carbone 14, dance and theatre, Montréal. 1993-1995
Client: Carbone 14
Location: 1345, avenue Lalonde, Montréal
Architects: Saucier + Perrotte architectes
Team: André Perrotte, Gilles Saucier, Frank Thonon, Yves Bouchard, Oscar Juarros, Robert d'Errico, Martin Bouchard, Jean Pelland.
Structural: Martoni, Cyr & Associés Inc.
Mechanical / electrical: Le groupe Teknika
Theatre consultant / construction manager: Scéno Plus Inc.

Université de Montréal, Faculty of Design, Montréal. 1994-1997
Client: Université de Montréal, Direction des Immeubles
Location: 2940, Ch. de la Côte Ste-Catherine, Montréal
Architects: Saucier + Perrotte architectes / Menkès Shooner Dagenais
Team: Gilles Saucier, Anik Shooner, René Menkes, André Perrotte, Yves Dagenais, Claudio Bardetti, Yves Bouchard, Alain Boudrias, Sarah Chouinard, Robert d'Errico, Andrew Dunbar, Pierre Gervais, Marie-Flore Gignac, Sonia Lambert, Alex Parmentier, Serge Poirier, Denise Saucier, Frank Thonon, Guy Trudel.
Structural: Nicolet, Chartrand, Knoll
Mechanical / electrical: Consortium ADS / Gareau
Landscape: Deshaies, Raymond / Blondin

Cinémathèque Québécoise, Museum of Video Arts and Exhibition Galleries, Montréal. 1994-1997
Client: Cinémathèque québécoise
Location: 335, Boul. de Maisonneuve Est, Montréal
Architects: Saucier + Perrotte architectes
Team: André Perrotte, Gilles Saucier, Martin Bouchard, Yves Bouchard, Robert d'Errico, Andrew Dunbar, Jean-François Lagacé, Lise Lachance, Pierre Colpron, Oscar Juarros, Frank Thonon
Structural: Le Groupe Teknika
Mechanical / electrical: Le Groupe Teknika / Dupras Ledoux

Collège Gérald-Godin, French College, Montréal. 1997-2000
Client: Collège Gérald-Godin
Location: 15 615, Boul. Gouin Ouest, Ste-Geneviève
Architects: Saucier + Perrotte architectes / Desnoyers Mercure architectes
Team: Gilles Saucier, André Perrotte, André J. Mercure, Yves Bouchard, Martin Bouchard, Robert d'Errico, Jean-François Lagacé, Jean-Olivier Nadeau, Marc-André Plourde, Pascale Tétrault, Yves Legris, Thanh Liem Nguyen, Luc Boivin, François Hogue, Ted Markis, Bernard Mercier
Structural: Génivel-BPR inc / Saia, Deslauriers et associés
Mechanical / electrical: Soprin-ADS
Landscape: Saint-Denis architectes paysagistes
Theatre consultant: Trizart

Central Park of Pudong, Montréal Pavilion, Shangai. 2000
Client: City of Montréal
Location: Central Park of Pudong, Shangai, People's Republic of China
Architects: Saucier + Perrotte architectes
Team: Gilles Saucier, André Perrotte, Julie Lafrenière, Yves Bouchard, Robert d'Errico, Jean-François Lagacé, Jean-Olivier Nadeau
Structural / mechanical / electrical: Dessau-Soprin
Landscape: Services des Parcs de la Ville de Montréal, Claude Cormier architectes paysagistes

Jardin Botanique, First Nations Garden Pavilion, Montréal. 2000
Client: Jardin Botanique de Montréal
Location: 4101 Rue Sherbrooke Est, Montréal, Québec
Architects: Saucier + Perrotte architectes
Team: Gilles Saucier, André Perrotte, Anna Bendix, Maxime-Alexis Frappier, Christian Hébert, Jean-François Lagacé, Sergio Morales
Structural / mechanical / electrical: Genivar
Museum consultant: Cultura - DES
Landscape: Williams Asselin Ackaoui et associés inc.

**McGill University, School of Music,
Montréal. 2001**

Client: McGillUniversity

Location: 555 Rue Sherbrooke Ouest, Montréal

Architects: Menkès Shooner Dagenais / Saucier + Perrotte
architectes

Conceptual design team: Gilles Saucier, Anik Shooner,
Maxime-Alexis Frappier, Caroline Elias, Marc-Antoine
Larose, Catherine Bélanger, Anna Bendix, Sudhir Suri,
Claudio Nunez

Project manager: Décarel inc.

Structural: Saia Deslauriers Kadanoff / Leconte
Brisebois Blais

Mechanical / electrical: Pellemon inc. / BPR

Acoustical consultant: Artec

**La Bordée, Theatre, Québec. 2000
(competition entry)**

Client: Le Théâtre de la Bordée

Location: Unbuilt

Architects: Saucier + Perrotte architectes

Team: Gilles Saucier, André Perrotte, Yves Bouchard,
Maxime-Alexis Frappier, Anna Bendix

3-D modeling: Mustang média

**Jyväskylä, Music and Arts Centre, Finland. 1998
(competition entry)**

Client: Music and Arts Centre, Jyväskylä

Location: Unbuilt

Architects: Saucier + Perrotte architectes

Team: Gilles Saucier, André Perrotte, Yves Bouchard,
Jean-Olivier Nadeau

**Leipziger Platz, Canadian Embassy, Berlin. 1999
(competition entry: finalist)**

Client: Government of Canada

Location: Unbuilt

Architects: Saucier + Perrotte architectes / Dunlop Farrow
architects (associate architects)

Team: Gilles Saucier, André Perrotte, Jean-François Lagacé,
Julie Lafrenière, Joseph Troppmann, Michael Moxam.

**Grande Bibliothèque du Québec, Library,
Montréal. 2001
(competition entry: finalist)**

Client: Grande Bibliothèque du Québec

Location: Unbuilt

Architects: Saucier + Perrotte architectes / Menkès
Shooner Dagenais

Design team: Gilles Saucier, André Perrotte, Anna Bendix,
Yves Bouchard, Maxime-Alexis Frappier, Yvon Lachance,
Julie Lafrenière

Landscape: Desvignes & Dalnoky, paysagistes; Michel Desvignes

Technological integration: Go Multimédia; Guy Desmarteaux

3-D modeling: Mustang média

Models: Atelier Glaf

**Concordia University, Arts-Engineering Building,
Montréal. 2001
(competition entry: finalist)**

Client: Concordia University

Location: Unbuilt

Architects: Saucier + Perrotte architectes /
NFOE architects

Team: Gilles Saucier, André Perrotte, Allen F. Onton,
Lucien Haddad, Anna Bendix, Christian Hébert,
Maxime-Alexis Frappier

Projects 1988 - 2002

2002	Orford, "New pavilion, Orford Arts Centre"
2002	Montréal, "New Arts Building" McGill University
2002	Montréal, "Boutique Michel Brisson" Michel Brisson
2002	Toronto, "Private residence"
2001	Toronto, "CCIT" University of Toronto
2001	Montréal, "Boutique Dubuc" Philippe Dubuc Designer
2001	Montréal, "Faculty of Music" McGill University
2001	Montréal, "Interior renovation" S. Bureau residence
2001	Toronto, "New College Residence" University of Toronto
2000	Waterloo, "Research laboratories" Perimeter Institute
2000	Longueuil, "Commercial building renovation" Claude Charpentier
2000	Montréal, "First Nations Garden Pavilion" Jardin Botanique Ville de Montréal
2000	Montréal, "Main Hall, James Building" McGill University
2000	Montréal, "New Stamps and Drawings Exhibition Gallery" Musée McCord
2000	Montréal, "Interior renovation, creative offices" Tube Image
2000	Montréal, "Production centre" Théâtre sans Fil
2000	Montréal, "Signage, Exhibition pavilion, Montreal Garden, Shanghai" Ville de Montréal
2000	Montréal, "Les lieux de la Couleur, Installation de Saucier+Perrotte" CCA
2000	Montréal, "Façade renovation" Réseau Admission
1999-2000	Montréal, "Private residence" J-M. Carpentier
2000	Montréal, "Interior renovation, Pollack Hall" McGill University
2000-2001	Montréal, "New exhibition space, interior renovation and studios" Musée McCord
1999-2000	Montréal, "New McGill Senate Board Chamber" McGill University
1999-2000	Shanghai, "Exhibition pavilion, Montreal Garden, Shanghai" Ville de Montréal
1999	Montréal, "Park services building" Caserne Letourneux
1999	Edmonton, "Signum Shop"
1999	Montréal, "Multipurpose room" Musée McCord
1999	Outremont, "Interior renovation" Vito Luprano
1998	Montréal, "Interior renovation" Résidence S. Bureau
1998	Outremont, "Interior renovation" Résidence Caroline Jamet
1998	Montréal, "Aménagement d'un salon de coiffure" Orbite
1998	Montréal, "Faculty of Music Building" McGill University
1997-2000	Sainte-Geneviève, "Gérald Godin College"
1997	Montréal, "Police Station" SPCUM
1997	Toronto, "Radix Showroom" Radix

Montréal, "Museum of Cinema – Cinémathèque Québécoise" — 1994-1997

Montréal, "CESAM, Centre for expertise and services in multimedia applications" MediaSphere Bell — 1996-1997

Montréal, "NAD Centre, School of Design and 3D Animation" — 1996-1997

Montréal, "CYCLONE Arts & Technologies, School of Computer Animation" — 1997

Montréal, "Interior renovation" Éclectic Salon — 1996

Outremont, "Restaurant Sarah Bernhardt" — 1996

Montréal, "Copper roof renovation, Allan Memorial Pavilion" Royal Victoria Hospital — 1996

Montréal, "Faculty of Design and Planning" Université de Montréal — 1994-1997

Montréal, "Phase IV Study, Université du Québec à Montréal" — 1995

Montréal, "Interior renovation" Cossette Communication /Marketing — 1994-1995

Ville LaSalle, "Salle Jean-Grimaldi" 800-seat theatre — 1994-1995

Montréal, Safety Standards "Judith-Jasmin Welcome Centre" — 1994-1995

Montréal, "Multi-Media Centre, Carbone 14-Prim" — 1993-1995

Montréal, Preliminary design "Faculty of Music, McGill University" McGill University — 1994

Montréal, Feasibility study "Cirque du Soleil Production Centre" — 1995

Montréal, "Residential complex, Faubourg-Québec" — 1993-1994

Longueuil, "Hall renovation," Groupe Mercille — 1993

Montréal, Feasibility study "Projet Faubourg-Québec" SHDM — 1992

Québec, "Orchestral shell – Grand Théâtre de Québec" — 1992-1993

Montréal, "University Garden – Université du Québec à Montréal" — 1993

Montréal, Preliminary design "Edifice pour la galerie Michel Tétrault", Rue Clark — 1992

Hudson, "Private residence" — 1991-1993

Bromont, "Preliminary design, residential project" — 1991

Montréal, Interior renovation "Dermatology Clinic" — 1991

Montréal, Theatre expansion "Théâtre Maisonneuve," Place des Arts — 1991

Longueuil, Renovation and addition "Cathédrale de Longueuil" — 1991

Montréal, Convertible space (240-300 seats) theatre "Théâtre d'Aujourd'hui," Rue St-Denis — 1990-91

Montréal, Acoustic renovation "Nouvelle Compagnie Théâtrale" — 1990

Montréal, 426-seat theatre "Théâtre du Rideau Vert", Rue St-Denis — 1990

Pont-Rouge, Golf club welcome centre study "Le Grand Portneuf" — 1990

Longueuil, Feasibility study for office complex "Place Charles-Lemoyne" — 1989

Montréal, Interior renovation "Carpentier Office" — 1989

Montréal, "Frontenac Street Workshop" — 1989

Montréal, Interior renovation, creative offices "Auger-Babeux/Publicité" — 1988

Montréal, Interior renovation "225 Rue Roy" — 1988

Awards

First Nations Garden Pavilion, Montréal,
OAQ Award of Excellence in Institutional Architecture — 2003

Boutique Michel Brisson, Montréal,
Grand Prize, Concours Commerce Design — 2003

Boutique Dubuc Mode de Vie, Montréal, Jury Grand Prize,
Concours Commerce Design — 2002

First Nations Garden Pavilion, Montréal, Governor General's Medal in Architecture — 2002

New College Residence, University of Toronto, Canadian Architect
Award of Excellence — 2001

Perimeter Institute, Waterloo, Architecture Magazine PA Award — 2001

College Gérald-Godin, OAQ Grand Prize
and Award of Excellence in Institutional Architecture — 2000

Orbite Salon, Honourable Mention, Commercial Design, OAQ — 2000

College Gérald-Godin, Prix Orange Rénovation "Sauvons Montréal" — 2000

First Nations Garden Pavilion, Montréal
and Exhibition Pavilion, Montreal Garden, Shanghai
Canadian Architect Award of Excellence — 2000

College Gérald-Godin, Canadian Architect Award of Excellence — 1999

Montréal and Exhibition Pavilion, Montreal Garden, Shanghai
Canadian Architect Award of Excellence — 1999

Orbite Salon, Jury and Public Grand Prize,
Concours Commerce Design — 1999

Cinémathèque Québécoise, Governor General's Medal of Merit in Architecture — 1999

Cinémathèque Québécoise, Award of Excellence for institutional architecture, OAQ — 1998

Résidence Mercille, Mention: residential architecture, OAQ — 1998

Cinémathèque Québécoise, Grand Prize, Canadian Interiors Award — 1998

Usine C, Carbone 14, Governor General's Medal of Merit in Architecture	1997
Eclectic Salon, Grand Prize, Concours Commerce Design Montréal	1997
Façade and entry hall, 2100 Drummond, Cossette Communication-Marketing, Honourable Mention, Concours Commerce Design Montréal	1996
Honourable Mention, OAQ	1995
Faculty of Design and Planning, Université de Montréal, Canadian Architect Award of Excellence	1995
Centre for Performing Arts, Carbone 14-Prim, Montréal, Mention en architecture OAQ.	1995
Centre for Performing Arts, Carbone 14-Prim, Montréal, Honourable Mention in Renovation / Recycling "Sauvons Montréal"	1995
Faculty of Design and Planning, Université de Montréal, The Art of CAD, first prize winner, Canadian Architect	1995
UQAM Phase IV Study, The Art of CAD, Honourable Mention, Canadian Architect	1995
Faculty of Music, McGill University, Canadian Architect Award of Excellence	1994
Montréal, "Concours pour le projet Faubourg-Québec" Winning Scheme	1993
Faculty of Design and Planning competition, l'Université de Montréal, Winning Scheme	1992
Montréal, "Théâtre du Rideau Vert" Rue St-Denis, Award of Excellence, l'Ordre des Architectes du Québec	1991
Centre du Théâtre d'Aujourd'hui Canadian Architect Award of Excellence	1990
Montréal, "Ateliers Municipaux de la Ville de Montréal" Jury Honourable Mention	1990
Montréal, "Rénovation du 225 est, rue Roy" Honourable Mention, l'Ordre des Architectes du Québec, Honourable Mention: recycling and renovation "Sauvons Montréal"	1989
Kitchener, "National Competition for the Design of the Kitchener City Hall" Finalist Project	1989

Bibliography

"First Nations Pavilion" and "Gérald Godin College", The Phaidon Atlas Of Contemporary World Architecture, Phaidon Press, 2004.

"Revealing Gesture", Azure Magazine, September/October 2003, Beth Kapusta, p.103-104.

"Architecture – Scénographies urbaines", Le Devoir, September 7 2003, Emmanuelle Vieira.

"Comme une seconde peau", Le Devoir, September 7 2003, Emmanuelle Vieira.

"Magic Lantern", Canadian Architect, June 2003, Ricardo L. Castro, p.24-27.

"Saucier + Perrotte en Ontario", Le Devoir, May 31 2003, Emmanuelle Vieira.

"Prix d'excellence en Architecture 2003", Jardins des Première Nations, La revue ARQ, May 2003, p.8.

"Taillé sur mesure", Azure Magazine, March/April 2003, Sylvie Berkowicz, p.66-69.

"Territoire intime d'une grande firme", La Presse, December 3 2002, Sophie Gironnay.

"Pavillon des Premières Nations au Jardin Botanique de Montréal", Architecture, July 2002, Julie Lasky, pp. 102-107.

"First Nations Garden Pavilion" Governor General's Medals in Architecture, Architecture Canada 2002, Tuns Press, pp. 92-99.

"Collège Gérald Godin, Montreal", l'ARCA, April 2002, Decio Guardigli. pp.30-37

"Faire bourlinguer son art", Le Devoir, February 3 2002, Louise-Maude Rioux Soucy.

"L'équipe montréalaise Saucier+Perrotte ar7chitectes se distingue sur la scène internationale", Le Devoir, February 3 2002, Louise-Maude Rioux Soucy.

"Perimeter Institute", 49th Annual P/A awards, Architecture, January 2002, pp. 90-91.

"Office house architects' design ideas", The Gazette, January 5 2002, Ricardo L. Castro.

"Award of Excellence: New College Residence, University of Toronto", Canadian Architect, December 2001, pp. 22-25.

"Collège Gérald Godin in Québec", Architectural Record, November 2001, Paul Byard, pp. 117-121.

"Shelter from the norm", The Globe and Mail, June 5 2001, Lisa Rochon.

"Newton's offspring", The Record, June 2 2001, Luisa D'Amato.

"Collège Gérald Godin – portion d'éternité", Intérieurs, April 2001, Diane Jutras, p. 85.

"La boîte à images de Montréal", Déco Architecture & Design, April 2001, Josiane Adib Torbey, pp. 42-44.

"Cinémathèque Québécoise, Montreal", Architectural Record, November 2000, Beth Kapusta, pp. 142-147.

"Un musée loin du folklore", La presse, November 6 2000, Jérome Delgado.

"Miracle in Montreal", Canadian Architect, August 2000, Kurt W. Forster, pp. 20-25.

"Something old, something new", The Globe and Mail, August 8 2000, Rhys Phillips.

"Beauty Clinic", The Architectural Review, June 2000, pp. 86-87.

"Saucier+Perrotte in Orbite", Canadian Interiors, May-June 2000, Rhys Phillips, pp. 53-54.

"A fine balance", Azure, May 2000, Beth Kapusta, pp. 80-82.

"Rubrique qui fait quoi", Intérieurs, April 2000, p. 18.

"Saucier+Perrotte primée", Journal Constructo, April 2000, Michel Valiquette.

"Cinq finalistes retenus pour la Grande Bibliothèque", La Presse, April 11 2000, Suzanne Colpron.

"Library architect's list down to five / Panel looks from Paris to B.C for Designers of Grande Bibliothèque du Québec", The Gazette, April 11 2000, Susan Semenak.

"Les finalistes sont connus / Concours d'architecture de la Grande Bibliothèque du Québec", Le Devoir, April 11 2000, Caroline Montpetit.

"Un nouveau collège / Un premier grand cru", Le Devoir, March 2000, Michèle Picard.

"Collège Gérald Godin-Taillé sur mesure pour l'industrie", Le Devoir, March 7 2000, Marie-Andrée Chouinard.

"À peine terminé, le cégep Gérald Godin est déjà primé", La Presse, March 4 2000, Claude Marsolais.

"Les honneurs pour Saucier+Perrotte", Journal Constructo, February 15 2000, Michel Valiquette.

"Un prix d'excellence décerné au Collège Gérald Godin", Journal Cités Nouvelles, February 2000, Lucie René.

"Award of Excellence: Collège Gérald Godin and Jardin de Montréal à Shanghaï", Canadian Architect, December 1999, pp. 30-31.

"Hairdressing salon wins for style", Canadian Interiors, November-December 1999, p. 10.

"Cinémathèque Québécoise à Montréal", Abitare, November 1999, Francesca Acerboni, pp. 176-177.

"Un Pavillon à Shanghaî", Le Devoir, November 27-28 1999, Jacques Martin.

"Montréal se paie une vitrine de prestige en Chine", Le Devoir, November 27-28 1999, François Cardinal.

"Shanghaï aura son Jardin de Montréal", La Presse, November 27 1999, Martine Roux.

"Shanghaï park is a model of pride", The Gazette, November 27 1999, Linda Gyulai.

"French Cégep joins old to new", The Gazette, November 27 1999, David Rose.

"Salon Orbite, Concours Commerce Design" L'Express D'Outremont, November 19 1999, Chantal Tittley.

"'In' designs are a cut above", The Gazette, October 28 1999, Annabelle King.

"Canadian Architect's October Update / Collège nearing completion", Canadian Architect, October 1999, p. 5.

"Rentrée réussie au cégep Gérald Godin", La Presse, October 15 1999, Martine Roux.

"L'affaire Berlin, Réflexion d'un architecte", Le Devoir, August 28-29 1999, Jacques Martin.

"Canadian Architect's August Update / IMCA Architects selected", Canadian Architect, August 1999, p.5.

"L'ancien monastère en voit de toutes les couleurs", La Presse, August 24 1999, Rima Elkouri.

"A Cégep roars to life", The Gazette, August 23 1999, Doug Sweet.

"What price flower diplomacy?", The Gazette, August 10 1999, Linda Gyulai.

"Motion & Pictures", Interior Design, July 1999, Monica Geran, pp. 136-141.

"A Berlin Chronicle", Canadian Architect, June 1999, Adèle Weder, pp.20-27.

"Montreal firm wins Calgary design bid", The Globe and Mail, June 19 1999, Adèle Weder.

"A distinct architecture", National Post, June 7 1999, Adèle Weder.

"La Cinémathèque Québécoise, Governor General's Medals", Canadian Architect, May 1999, pp. 32.

"Cinémathèque Québécoise", Governor General's Medals in Architecture, Architecture Canada 1999, Tuns Press, pp. 130-137.

"Ambassade du Canada à Berlin", Azure, June 1999, John Ota, pp. 26-27.

"Salon Orbite, Commerce Design Montréal", Intérieurs, April 1999, Odile Hénault, pp. 62-63.

"Un nouveau salon en orbite", Clin d'Oeil, March 1999, p. 141.

"Ottawa's reasons for Berlin's embassy choice challenged", National Post, March 19 1999, Adèle Weder.

"Clothes encounter", Azure, January 1999, Beth Kapusta, pp. 34-35.

"Le temps des couleurs, le nouveau salon orbite", Le Devoir, December 4-5 1998, Jacques Martin.

"Correspondent's file", Architecture Record, December 1998, Beth Kapusta, pp. 31-34.

"Invitation à l'éveil", Intérieurs, November 1998, Hubert Beringer, pp. 36-40.

"Collage of life " World Architecture, October 1998, Katherine Macinnes, pp. 64-67.

"Moving image", The Architectural Review, August 1998, Brian Carter, pp. 74-77.

"Un havre entre l'ancien et le nouveau", Le Devoir, August 22-23 1998, Jacques Martin.

"Critique. A silk purse from a sow's ear", Canadian Architect, May 1998, Odile Hénault, pp. 30-33.

"Cinema noir", Azure, March-April 1998, Adèle Weder, pp. 44-47.

"Usine C / Carbone 14," Governor General's Medals in Architecture, Architecture Canada 1997, Tuns Press, pp. 154-161.

"A cinematic take on space", The Globe and Mail, April 19 1997, Beth Kapusta.

"Film centre gets a stimulating makeover", The Gazette, March 8 1997, Ricardo L. Castro.

"Cinémathèque Québécoise reopens after $16-million facelift", The Gazette, February 26 1997, Alan Hustak.

"La Cinémathèque fait peau neuve, Ouverture de la nouvelle Cinémathèque", La Presse, February 26 1997, Luc Perreault.

"La Cinémathèque québécoise a rouvert ses portes hier", Le Journal de Montréal, February 26 1997, Marie Plourde.

"Une image dépoussiérée", Le Journal de Montréal, February 26 1997, Louise Blanchard.

"Pour la nouvelle Cinémathèque, Oscars, Césars, Love, etc.", Le Devoir, February 22-23 1997, Sophie Gironnay.

"Saucier et Perrotte: les architectes du spectacle", Le Journal de Montréal, February 17 1997, Jean-Guy Martin.

"Awards, Footnotes and Backstories", Canadian Architect, December 1996, Donald McKay, p. 20.

"Flowing with the transparent office", The Globe and Mail, October 12 1996, Gary Michael Dault.

"Canadian Architect, Interior Architecture", Canadian Architect, October 1996, Beth Kapusta, pp. 30-33.

"Urban Communications Urbaines", Architecture + Design INSITE, May 1996, pp. 59-61.

"Canadian Architect, Theatre 1: Production Factory", Canadian Architect, March 1996, Beth Kapusta, pp. 20-23.

"Canadian Architect , House 1: The Dynamics of an Ideal Villa", Canadian Architect, February 1996, Beth Kapusta, pp. 17-21.

"Award of Excellence: Université de Montréal, Faculté de l'Aménagement", Canadian Architect, December 1995, pp. 24-25.

"La revue du Pixel d'or: lauréats 1995", Omer DeSerres, September 1995, p. 22.

"Competition: The Art of CAD", First Prize Winner: Université de Montréal, Faculté d'Aménagement, July 1995, pp. 18-21.

"Zwei Theater in Montréal", Baumeister Munchen, April 1995, Amber Sayah, pp. 38-43.

"Usine C, une véritable oeuvre d'art pour Carbone 14", La Presse, March 30 1995, Jean Beaunoyer.

"Being at home with Carbone", La Presse, March 30 1995, Nathalie Petrowski.

"Les murs de Carbone 14", Le Devoir, March 28 1995, Sophie Gironnay.

"En avant la Musique", Le Devoir, February 4-5 1995, Sophie Gironnay.

"La ménagerie de verre", Le Devoir, January 14-15 1995, Sophie Gironnay.

"Award of excellence: McGill University Faculty of Music and Opera house", The Canadian Architect, December 1994, pp. 32-34.

"University showcases architectural bequest", The Globe and Mail, December 3 1994, Adele Freedman.

"Timely elegance", Bar addition to Théâtre Maisonneuve, Place des Arts, The Canadian Architect, September 1993, pp. 36-38.

"Montreal Scene 1, Montreal Scene 2", Architectural Review, May 1993, pp. 80-84.

"Bureaux d'architectes", La revue ARQ, April 1993, Gilles Saucier, p. 13.

"Architects invite public to look in", The Gazette, January 23 1993, Ricardo L. Castro.

"Montreal Moderns: Two Theatres on St-Denis", The Canadian Architect, September 1992, Bruce Anderson, pp. 14-20.

"Theatre injects note of 'realism' into architecture scene", The Gazette, February 29 1992, Ricardo L. Castro.

"Quand un petit théâtre remporte un grand prix d'architecture", La Presse, December 1 1991, Jean-Pierre Bonhomme.

"Les prix d'excellence 1991",Théâtre du Rideau Vert, Le Devoir, November 16 1991, Odile Hénault.

"Pour une vision urbaine du théâtre", La revue ARQ, August 1991, Susan Ross, pp. 8-15.

"Théâtre du Rideau Vert makeover a triumph of critical modernism", The Gazette, February 2 1991, Ricardo L. Castro.

"Award of Excellence: Centre du Théâtre d'Aujourd'hui", The Canadian Architect, December 1990, pp. 22-23.

"Eight young firms", The Canadian Architect, September 1990, pp. 20-21.

"Competing Visions", The Kitchener City Hall Competition, The Melting Press, Detlef Mertins, Virginia Wright, pp. 86-93.

"Kitchener's new municipal center", Architectural Record, January 1990, pp. 30-31.

"Les prix d' excellence de l'OAQ 1989 : Le 225 rue Roy est", La revue ARQ, December 1989, p. 19.

"Kitchener City Hall national architectural design competition", La revue ARQ, December 1989, pp. 24-25.

"Kitchener City Hall Competition", The Canadian Architect, November 1989, p. 38.

"Neo-modernism could be architectural trend of the '90s", The Gazette, November 18 1989, Ricardo L. Castro.

"Montreal's architecture in the 1980's, Resisting practices or the practice of resistance", La revue ARQ, August 1989, Ricardo L. Castro, pp. 30-33.

"Voilà the craftsmen-architects", Azure, July-August 1989, Odile Hénault, p. 9.

"Cinema provides inspiration for imaginative interior design", The Gazette, July 22 1989, Anna Mainella.

"Les projets d'excellence ARQ 1989", La revue ARQ, June 1989, pp. 15, 20.

"Ce ne sont plus les peintres qui annoncent les nouvelles formes", La Presse, April 30 1989, Jean-Pierre Bonhomme.

Drawings and Photography Credits

Drawings

Mustang Médias
106, 108, 120, 126, 129

Bernard St-Denis
58

Other drawings composed and formatted
by Saucier + Perrotte

Photography

Brigitte Desrochers
82

Marc Cramer
2, 3, 4, 5, 12, 19, 56, 62, 63 (top right, bottom left)
66, 67, 69, 69, 72, 73, 85, 90, 91, 92, 93, 97 (left)

Wendy Graham
71, 81

Paul Labelle
102

Alain Laforest
28, 29, 32 (bottom), 33, 41, 101, 123, 124-125, 128

Jacques Lavoie
24, 27, 32 (top left)

Jean-François Lenoir
42 (bottom), 50 (right)

Éric Piché
15, 34, 42, 43, 44, 47, 48, 49, 50 (left), 51, 54, 55,
99, 100, 103

Ben Rahn
74

Other photographs by Saucier + Perrotte

Contributors

Brian Carter

Brian Carter is an architect who worked in practice with Arup Associates in London prior to joining the University of Michigan, where he was Chair of Architecture from 1994 to 2001. He is currently Dean of the School of Architecture & Urban Planning at the State University of New York at Buffalo. His work has been published in numerous international journals, including Casabella, Detail and Architectural Review. The author of several books, Brian Carter also initiated the MAP series, which won an AIA International Book Award.

Essy Baniassad

Essy Baniassad, as former Dean of the Faculty of Architecture at The Technical University of Nova Scotia (now Dalhousie University), founded Tuns Press and initiated the Documents in Canadian Architecture series. He is currently the Chair and Professor in the Department of Architecture at the Chinese University of Hong Kong.

Stéphane Huot

Stéphane Huot is an independent graphic designer/publisher working in Montréal. He graduated from Rhode Island School of Design with a MFA in graphic design in 1996. He has been a part-time teacher at Université du Québec à Montréal's School of Design since 1997.

Georges Adamczyk

Georges Adamczyk is Professor and Head of the School of Architecture at Université de Montréal. He was director of the Environmental Design Program (1977-1982), director of the Art History program (1982-1983) and director of the Design Department (1984-1989) at Université du Québec à Montréal. From 1993 to June 1999, he was also Director of the Design Centre at UQAM. He is a collaborator of the research group LEAP (Laboratoire d'étude de l'architecture potentielle) and a member of the editorial board of ARQ, Architecture Quebec.

Louis-Charles Lasnier

Louis-Charles Lasnier studied graphic design in Montréal and architecture at the University of Waterloo. He worked for Bruce Mau Design, Claude Cormier Landscape Architects and Saucier + Perrotte before opening his own studio. As an exhibition designer, his clients include the Canadian Centre for Architecture and the Faculté d'Aménagement de l'Université de Montréal. He teaches at Université du Québec à Montréal's School of Design.

Acknowledgements

The preparation and publication of this monograph have involved many people and without their support and cooperation neither would have been possible. My thanks are first and foremost to Essy Baniassad, who has continued to enthusiastically support this series of monographs on the new and inspiring architecture in Canada, initiated in 1994. His advice, energy, thoughtful criticism and generous contributions of time, ideas and words have been invaluable over the years and especially critical to the making of this book. With that encouragement, particular thanks must go to Gilles Saucier and André Perrotte and their colleagues in the office, firstly for their inspiration, hard work and persistence in designing and overseeing the construction of a series of splendid buildings. They demonstrate a belief in the importance of design and have helped not only to reconstruct the city and the region but also to advance the cultural life of French Canada. Without those buildings there would be no reason to make a book. Some of the same pre-occupations have informed the preparation of the book and they have also given most generously of their time and skills to assemble existing information and prepare new material especially for this publication. In this context particular thanks is due to Louis-Charles Lasnier and Stéphane Huot, whose insights, patience and tireless efforts to translate ideas into material and material into print have made the book realizable.

The hard work and steadfast reliability of Donald Westin of Tuns Press continues to make the books in this series and others by Tuns Press possible. Thanks must also go to Professor Georges Adamczyk at the Université de Montréal for his thoughtful contributions and insightful postscript, and to Rita Cloghesy for her translation of that postscript. Professor Thomas Emodi and Dean Grant Wanzel both offered encouragement in Halifax, and Annette W. LeCuyer created space for me to work on this project in Buffalo and London.

The publication of this monograph has been made possible with financial support made available through The Canada Council and with the unfailing assistance, enthusiasm and resources of the Faculty of Architecture and Planning at Dalhousie University.   BC

Other publications by Tuns Press

Architecture Canada 2004 : The Governor General's
Medals for Architecture
ISBN 0-929112-51-2, 2004

Wood Design Awards 2003
ISBN 0-929112-54-0, 2003

Barry Johns Architects : Selected Projects 1984-1998
ISBN 0-929112-32-6, 2000

Brian MacKay-Lyons : Selected Projects 1986-1997
ISBN 0-929112-39-3, 1998

Works : The Architecture of A.J. Diamond,
Donald Schmitt & Company, 1968-1995
ISBN 0-929112-31-8, 1996

Patkau Architects : Selected Projects 1983-1993
ISBN 0-929112-28-8, 1994

For additional information, please see our website:
tunspress.dal.ca